Being uncommon in to [...]
men of all ages have a [...]
Let's all work to be unc [...]

CAM CAMERON
Offensive coordinator, [...]

Finally, a book for dads and sons! In my eighteen years of working with men, one of the most often asked questions I hear is, "Is there anything I can read with my son?" Now the answer is, "Yes, read *Playbook for an Uncommon Life*." This book can be read by a father and son and provide jumping off points for weeks of discussion on the important issues of life and what it means to be a man in today's world. I can't wait to read it with my sons.

STEVE SONDERMAN
Men's ministry pastor, Elmbrook Church, and
founder of No Regrets Men's Ministry

I found each chapter of *Playbook for an Uncommon Life* meaty and very important for young men today in particular. This book is a must-read for fathers who have sons and if the sons are of an age that they would understand the content, to read and discuss it with them chapter by chapter. If I had to pick one chapter to focus upon, it would be chapter 7, "Respect Authority." In roughly three pages, Coach Dungy teaches the importance of respecting authority whether it seems fair or not. As he says, in years to come most young men will see the wisdom of doing so. This could not be more timely since we live in an age of severe disrespect for authority in our country by far too many young people. Coach Dungy is clearly an honest, loving, Christ-centered man with a passion and a mission to help young men before it is too late. I applaud him for doing so.

BOB MCCOOK
President, Priority One Foundation

WELCOME to the *Playbook for an Uncommon Life*!

Playbook for an Uncommon Life contains selections from each chapter of Tony Dungy's bestselling book *Uncommon*. It is perfectly suited to be read on its own or to be used as a participant's guide for Tony Dungy's *Dare to Be Uncommon*, a four-week character-building DVD curriculum.

If you are reading this book in conjunction with the DVD curriculum, we recommend the following schedule, reading the chapters listed *before* each session in order to maximize impact:

Session 1: Cultivating Uncommon Character—
chapters 1–4

Session 2: The Power of Positive Influence—
chapters 5–11

Session 3: Reaching Your Full Potential—
chapters 12–22

Session 4: Living with Purpose—chapters 23–31

Regardless of how you use this book, we hope that you will live a life of significance and dare to be uncommon!

Tyndale House Publishers

PLAYBOOK
FOR AN
UNCOMMON
LIFE

**SELECTIONS FROM
THE *NEW YORK TIMES*
BESTSELLER *UNCOMMON***

TONY DUNGY

WITH NATHAN WHITAKER

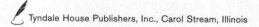 Tyndale House Publishers, Inc., Carol Stream, Illinois

TYNDALE and Tyndale's quill logo are registered trademarks of Tyndale House Publishers, Inc.

Dare to Be Uncommon and the Dare to Be Uncommon logo are trademarks of Tyndale House Publishers, Inc.

Playbook for an Uncommon Life

Copyright © 2010 by Tony Dungy. All rights reserved.

This book is adapted from *Uncommon: Finding Your Path to Significance*, copyright © 2009 by Tony Dungy.

Cover photo of Tony Dungy taken by Stephen Vosloo. Copyright © by Tyndale House Publishers, Inc. All rights reserved.

Football play diagram copyright © blackred/iStock. All rights reserved.

Designed by Erik Peterson

Published in association with the literary agency of Legacy, LLC, Winter Park, Florida 32789.

Unless otherwise indicated, all Scripture quotations are taken from the *Holy Bible*, New Living Translation, copyright © 1996, 2004, 2007 by Tyndale House Foundation. Used by permission of Tyndale House Publishers, Inc., Carol Stream, Illinois 60188. All rights reserved.

Scripture quotations marked NIV are taken from the Holy Bible, *New International Version,*® *NIV.*® Copyright © 1973, 1978, 1984 by Biblica, Inc.™ Used by permission of Zondervan. All rights reserved worldwide. www.zondervan.com.

ISBN 978-1-4143-4550-5 (softcover)
ISBN 978-1-4143-6706-4 (6-pack)

Printed in the United States of America

15   14   13   12
7   6   5   4

A MESSAGE FROM TONY DUNGY

The highway to hell is broad, and its gate is wide for the many who choose that way. But the gateway to life is very narrow and the road is difficult, and only a few ever find it.

MATTHEW 7:13-14

IT'S A HARD THING TO be a man today. It's especially hard to be a young man with character. It's all too easy to follow the crowd, to take the easy path—and find destruction.

That's why I wrote this book. I've seen far too many young men choose that wrong path. I wanted to encourage young men that what they see played out on TV and in the lives of those around them doesn't have to be their life. God calls us to great things. He calls us to lives of significance.

He calls us to be *uncommon*.

Being uncommon often means choosing the hard path, but it always means choosing the better one. Jesus knew what He was talking about when He said, "The highway to hell is broad . . . but the gateway to life is very narrow and the road is difficult."

I wrote *Playbook for an Uncommon Life* (and the larger book from which it is taken, *Uncommon*) to give you advice from someone a little farther down the road. I've tried to choose the right paths in my life, though I haven't always succeeded, and my hope is that through my successes and failures I can help you find—and stay on—the good paths and avoid the bad ones.

Each chapter in this playbook focuses on one characteristic of what it means to be an uncommon man. At the start of each chapter, I've included a quote from someone who gets that characteristic right to encourage you that you aren't walking this path alone. I've also highlighted a key idea from each chapter to help you think about what that characteristic might look like in your own life.

I can't guarantee the uncommon life will be easy, but I can assure you that it's worth it. I invite you to start today. Step out from the crowd. Stand up for what's right.

Be uncommon.

CONTENTS

INTRODUCTION

Not all those who wander are lost.

J. R. R. TOLKIEN

SINCE COMING TO INDIANAPOLIS, I have become friends with two young men. They grew up fairly close to each other, but were raised in different circumstances. Brandon Robinson is white. He grew up in a two-parent home in rural Indiana. Dallas Clifton is black and was raised by his mother in Indianapolis.

But both boys have a lot in common. Both are bright and articulate and have engaging personalities. Both are good hearted and good looking. But Brandon and Dallas have another thing in common. Both are in prison.

Brandon was raised in a quiet neighborhood in Warsaw, Indiana. His parents were loving and supportive, wanted the best for him, and tried to keep him away from negative influences. But Brandon began experimenting with marijuana and alcohol. It seemed harmless, until one summer night. It was just a short ride on a road Brandon knew very well. But he failed to stop; entered the intersection at sixty miles per hour in his pickup; hit a car; and killed three people, seriously injuring two others. His actions were caused by a blood alcohol level well above Indiana's legal limit. He was sentenced to twenty-eight years in prison.

Three people's lives ended, and the lives of the two surviving passengers, and all the families, forever changed at that moment.

Alicia Clifton knew Dallas was special. Dallas's sister played the piano, and he often imitated her. By age four, he was playing with both hands, and he progressed quickly. By fifteen, he was playing classical music, writing his own songs, and winning talent contests around Indianapolis.

But Alicia began to worry about Dallas. She knew he was paid well for his playing, but he seemed to have too much money at times. She later discovered that Dallas was gambling. She warned Dallas about the chances he was taking. But everything was going so well for Dallas, he was sure his mom was worrying for no reason.

After high school, Dallas enrolled in a university in Kentucky on a music scholarship. He returned to Indianapolis during a break and found a dice game to pass the time. When he lost about $200, he borrowed it from another player, feeling sure his luck would change. But it didn't. Not only had he lost *his* money, but he had also lost the money he borrowed.

Dallas had to return to school, but the "friend" who loaned him the money told him that if he didn't get the money from him, he would get it from his family, one way or another.

Dallas had a problem. He could have tried to borrow from someone else, or he could have asked his mother or someone at church for help. But he didn't. He knew that most people in the underground gambling world kept large sums with them. He got a gun and held up someone who was leaving another dice game. He knew it wasn't the right thing to do, but he figured it was the only way he could protect his family. At the age of nineteen, this promising young man was sentenced to five years in prison.

Brandon and Dallas were really my motivation to write this book. Two young men, two different backgrounds and upbringings. Both ended up in prison. It's not an inner-city, economic, or even a religious problem. The kind of ideas young people are buying into and the pressure to conform are causing them to follow the path of least resistance.

Sadly, that seems to be the path that many of us naturally take. Things are accepted as normal without any thought as to whether they should be or whether there might be a better way. Too often we resign ourselves to accepting that things just are the way they are.

Young men today are told to demand respect, take no prisoners whether on the streets or in bed, look out for number one. But what does it really mean to *be a man*?

You were created to be more. The messages of the world are a cop-out: the messages of sexual conquest, of financial achievement, of victory in general. Not only are these messages not fair, but they also fall so far short of who you can be.

I hope this book will help you think about where you're headed. Often the path isn't clear. I realize that many of these topics are complex. And you'll probably notice that most of my thoughts come from what I believe the Bible says it takes to be a man. I won't apologize for or shy away from that, because God's Word has always been the best source of advice for me.

At the end of the day, I'm sure of one thing: accumulating stuff and women and titles and money are the wrong keys to the good life. Fitting in, following the crowd, and being common are not what we're supposed to do. There's more in store for us.

Cal Stoll, one of my coaches, often told me, "Success is uncommon, therefore not to be enjoyed by the common man. I'm looking for uncommon people."

That should be true for the rest of us as well. Over the next pages, I hope we can figure out what it means to be a man. A true man, one who is *uncommon*.

PART I

DEVELOP
YOUR CORE

Experience is the
name everyone gives
to their mistakes.
OSCAR WILDE

KEYS FOR DEVELOPING YOUR CORE

1. Remember that what you do when no one is watching matters.

2. The means matter as much as the ends, if not more.

3. Hang in there. Character is revealed through adversity.

4. Truth is critical. Being truthful is too.

5. You are important, but not indispensable. The same goes for others. See yourself as a significant part of the process.

6. Be careful what you do with your resources, gifts, time, and talents. You've been entrusted with them.

7. Life is hard. Courage is essential.

CHAPTER 1

CHARACTER

Educating the mind without educating the heart is no education at all.

ARISTOTLE

CHARACTER IS A QUALITY THAT can be measured just like height, weight, and speed. In fact, when I was coach of the Indianapolis Colts, we put more emphasis on character than on a player's physical tools. Coaching ability or talent cannot make up for a lack of character. In the draft, there are only a few things that would knock a player out of consideration for our team, and this issue of character was one of them. We had a category on our evaluation form labeled DNDC—*Do Not Draft because of Character*. Every year, players we put in that category were drafted in the first round by other teams, and some even went on to become household names in the NFL. But we passed on them because we saw something in their character that made us believe they were not worth the risk. Most of the time, we were right.

That's not necessarily the common approach

today, though. Results are emphasized so much that it seems not to matter how you get them. Moving up is considered more important than *the way* you move up. It doesn't matter what kind of person you are, just what you can do as a player. It doesn't matter if you follow the rules or break them, just as long as you come out on top. After all, that's what everyone will remember at the end of the day. With this approach, competitors think: *Everyone is doing it, so to have a real chance at success, I have to do it too, right?*

That approach is why we have steroid testing in the NFL and MLB. That's why Olympic medals are forfeited. Here's the truth: *What I do is not as important as how I do it.* Pay attention to this and make sure you get it right. How you play, and how you live, are more important than what you accomplish. These words keep coming back to me when I am tempted to choose what is expedient over what is right.

> **How you play, and how you live, are more important than what you accomplish.**

Athletes who bend the rules to get ahead usually get caught in the long run. But even if they don't get caught, they will always know how they made it to the top. Deep down they'll know that they're frauds, and they'll wonder if they actually had what it took to accomplish their achievements on a fair, level playing field.

And even if you finish your athletic career without a scandal, at some point in life you'll come up against somebody who *does* care how the game is played. It might be a boss or board of directors or even your own family. They'll be asking: Can you be counted on to do things the right way? Do you have the appropriate habits to get you through a tough situation, or are you the type to cut corners and hope things turn out all right? Your character will determine the answer.

Character begins with the little things in life. You must show that you can be trusted with each and every thing, no matter how trivial it may seem. You have to know what is right, and you have to choose to do it. Your actions must reflect an inner life committed to honor and uncompromising integrity.

In a common world, becoming an uncommon man begins by cultivating uncommon character.

CHAPTER 2

HONESTY AND INTEGRITY

Honesty is the first chapter in the book of wisdom.

THOMAS JEFFERSON

WHEN I WAS GROWING UP, the rules in our home were set in stone. If there was a rule, we knew we had better follow it. An interesting corollary, however, was that honesty had a way of reducing any punishment to come. As a boy, I thought that my dad had coined the phrase "the truth shall set you free," but when I got older, I learned he was actually quoting Jesus.

Skirting the rules will come back to hurt you. Whether it's doing something illegal or cheating on a test rather than actually learning the material, you may get the edge and experience a short-term "win," but dishonesty will eventually catch up with you. I'm fortunate to have learned this at home. When I went away to college, my mother's words kept coming back to me: *It's sometimes easier to do the wrong thing, but it's always better to do the right thing.* That's life. That's integrity—the choice between what's convenient and what's right.

Integrity is what you do when no one is watching. It's doing the right thing all the time, even when it may work to your disadvantage. Integrity is keeping your word. Integrity is that internal compass and rudder that directs you to where you know you should go when everything around you is pulling you in a different direction.

Integrity is critical to everything we do because it is the foundation of trustworthiness in our own eyes, in the eyes of those around us, and in God's eyes. Can I count on you to be my teammate, perform your assignment, and do your work in the weight room in the off-season? Can I count on you to be my business partner, or do I have to keep one eye on you while I'm trying to serve the customers? Can I count on you to do what you say you will do, no matter what may come along to make it difficult?

If you're still living at home, can your parents trust you to do the right thing all of the time, even when they're not there? When you get married, will your wife be able to count on you to be her faithful husband? Or will she have to worry about you having an affair because you aren't honest in other areas of your life?

The great thing about integrity is that it has nothing to do with wealth or race or gender or accomplishments. From the moment you are born, you—and you alone—determine whether you will be a person of integrity. Integrity does not come in degrees—low, medium, or high. You either have integrity or you do not.

You can read in the Old Testament book of Daniel (chapter 6) that Daniel "was faithful, always responsible, and completely trustworthy." We should live our lives like Daniel, so that if we ever had an FBI background check or a newspaper reporter digging into our personal lives, they would find no "dirt" on us but would find us to be honest and trustworthy.

> Integrity is doing the right thing all the time.

I care about my reputation, but I can't control what other people think about me. What I *can* control is my integrity: what *I* think of me. I do this by taking care of the little things, day in and day out, even when no one else is watching.

CHAPTER 3

HUMILITY AND STEWARDSHIP

We can't all be heroes because somebody has to sit on the curb and clap as they go by.

WILL ROGERS

MORE AND MORE, AS NEW players come into the league each year, I see what appears to be a "look at me" attitude. It doesn't seem to be driven by ego as much as by a struggle to survive in a world with a finite number of positions, where so many stand ready to take your place. It's further driven into them that the more "*SportsCenter* moments" they have, the more they will be worth to their team—and the more money they'll get paid. Guys will justify their attitudes by saying that if they don't blow their own horns, nobody will.

The problem is that nobody really listens when we blow our own horns; after all, we're biased. Also, it's pretty unbecoming. I think that's why my mother always told me never to do it. She may have been thinking of Proverbs 27:2, which says, "Let someone else praise you, not your own mouth—a stranger, not your own lips."

We claim that we like the quiet, humble athlete, but those aren't the guys who get the focus—at least not as much as the guys trying to bring attention to their own names. Barry and Deion Sanders came into the NFL together in 1989. Barry was "old school." He did his job and played spectacular football, and when he scored a touchdown, he handed the ball to the official and went back to the bench.

After games, it was hard to get him to talk about himself. He would praise his offensive linemen, then stay away from the cameras as much as possible. As great as Barry Sanders was, the media tended to gravitate more toward Deion Sanders, the self-proclaimed "Prime Time." Deion was flashy, loud, and proud. He played great and was always ready to put on a show, especially for the cameras. Behind the scenes, Barry and Deion probably weren't much different. Everyone who played with Deion said he was hardworking, a great teammate, and not really like the "Prime Time" persona he was known for. But Deion had figured out that flash sells. He had endorsements, shoe and clothing lines, and notoriety.

But there's a problem with this. Proverbs 16:18 says, "Pride goes before destruction." Time and time again we see examples where the fine line between confidence and pride has been blurred, resulting in fall after fall. Pride is all about me, but confidence is a realization that God has given me abilities and created me to fill a unique role that no one else is called to fill. Borne in humility, confidence is a recognition that life is not about me but about using the gifts and abilities I have been blessed with to their fullest. And it's not just using the gifts to benefit me, but to help my team and impact others.

I appreciate that form of humility. It's not a false modesty, claiming that what you accomplished or who you are isn't important, but a realization that God created all of us with unique gifts and abilities. It's a different dynamic than tearing myself down; it's trying to lift others up. Once you can do that, it becomes much easier to let go of status or false ideas of respect.

Rather than insisting that others respect us, we need to make sure that *we* are respecting *others*, holding *others* in the proper esteem. Those who truly live out that quality will make the best spouses, teammates, parents, friends, and business partners. Are you modeling that for those who look up to you? Hopefully you're teaching them that humility is to be valued.

Chuck Noll, football Hall of Fame coach of the Pittsburgh Steelers from 1969 to 1991 and winner of four Super Bowls, gave me my start in the NFL, both as a player and later as a coach. Coach Noll had a great way of keeping everything in perspective on those legendary Steeler teams of the 1970s. He used to assure us both with words and by the way he treated us that every player was important, but he also made it clear that no one was indispensable. We knew that if one of our star players was injured, we could still play well and still win. So even though we had many Hall of Fame players, our games were never about individual accomplishments. Teamwork was valued above all.

This was the primary reason that Coach Noll brought in assistant coaches from the college ranks. Similarly, when he traded players away (like me!), he always looked to get draft picks in return, not players from other teams. He wanted people who would buy into the "Steeler Way" and not try to bring other ideas into play. Other teams may have good ideas that work well for them, but we would win the Steeler Way. And every Steeler believed that, which is one of the reasons we were so successful.

None of us was ever left thinking that he was the most important piece of the puzzle, but rather that he was a significant piece and that every piece was an important and necessary element to achieve the team's goals. I've found over the years that such a perspective is a much healthier and less pressurized way to view myself: important but not indispensable.

It seems a very natural progression from discussing humility to talking about stewardship. Stewardship—like humility—requires a recognition that life is not about us. Specifically, a clear understanding of stewardship not only recognizes that it is not about us but also believes that it is all about God and that everything belongs to and comes from God. This sounds good and is certainly something we can all embrace—at least intellectually—but allowing stewardship to direct the decisions of daily living . . . Well, that is another matter entirely.

For example, what kind of car have you recently purchased? What do you give to your church? What ministries or charities have you recently donated to? The old saying "show me your checkbook and I'll tell you what's important to you" still rings true today. Where we put our money is one of the telltale indicators as to whether we understand the concept of stewardship.

But stewardship does not just apply to money. It's also about time. What do we do with the twenty-four hours a day we've been given? Stewardship is also about our talents and abilities. What have we done to maximize the gifts and abilities we find within ourselves?

> **Rather than insisting that others respect us, we need to make sure that *we* are respecting *others*.**

Don't get me wrong; I don't have it down as well as I should. I probably never will. Some of the men I've been fortunate to work with in football through the years are far better examples of good stewardship than I am. Their examples haunt me, but they also inspire me. I still have a tendency to make poor choices with my time, procrastinate about improving some area of my life, and hold on to things too tightly as if I owned them, fearing that if I open my hands they will fly away. I should know better, yet I'm continuing to learn that stewardship is not the same as ownership, and it's definitely not about me.

We begin to approach a true understanding of what stewardship is when we realize that everything we have is a gift from God. We are His, and the things we have in our control are His resources *entrusted* to us—for wise usage. Perhaps, I would even add, for *eternal* usage. When we begin to see ourselves as the stewards or trustees of the resources we control—not the owners—we are on the verge of understanding the true meaning of stewardship, whether those resources are our bodies, abilities, time, or possessions. So if it all comes from Him, I suppose one of the questions He might be asking is this: "Can you be trusted with what I gave you?"

In order to answer that question, you'll need to ask yourself several more: How do I use what I have? Can I be trusted with more? Do I take care of the body He has given me? Do I need a thirty-hour day, or do I simply need to be more efficient and incorporate better priorities in the twenty-four hours I've been given?

And finally, as stewards of all we have within our control, we must ask, Do I invest it in eternity? Do I do things that will outlive me? Do I invest in the lives of others? Do I invest in the expansion of God's agenda?

Stewardship—it's all about Him.

CHAPTER 4

COURAGE

Twenty years from now you will be more disappointed by the things you didn't do than by the ones you did do. So throw off the bowlines. Sail away from the safe harbor. Catch the trade winds in your sails. Explore. Dream. Discover.

MARK TWAIN

ONE OF THE MOST IMPORTANT things I have learned is having the courage to stand by my convictions—those things I know are right, those guiding principles I know to stick with. Sometimes that means standing out or not being popular, but sometimes that's the only responsible place to be. It doesn't make the days any easier, but at least I feel like I'm still heading in the right direction.

My parents had always made it clear that my siblings and I were going to college. There were times when it set us apart. Studying was necessary, both to earn good grades and to learn the material we would later need for college work. This sometimes put me at odds with my friends, many of whom weren't planning to go to college. They wanted me to play ball or just have fun. My parents were okay with those things, but only *after* studying. They set up the rules for me because I didn't always have the courage to say, "I can't hang out now; I need to study." It was easier to say, "My parents won't let me." But eventually, I would have to stand up on my own.

No one is immune to peer pressure, and we're susceptible to it at any age. It's just that as we get older, we do a better job of rationalizing or hiding it. But through the years, I've learned a way to deal with it: I make sure I know for myself what is right and am prepared to stick with it. Courage can be demonstrated by standing up to the school bully or intervening to prevent someone you don't know from being hurt. But more often it's the day-to-day moments of reaching inside yourself to find the courage to stand alone that can be the toughest.

> **I make sure I know for myself what is right and am prepared to stick with it.**

When I was a first-year coach, I was advised to be myself. For me, that meant I could continue to live out my life as a Christian on a daily basis as I coached. "God gives you convictions for a reason," the team's owner told me.

Stand by your convictions. Summon the courage to be uncommon.

PART II

LOVE
YOUR FAMILY

Be who you are and say
what you feel, because
those who mind don't
matter and those who
matter don't mind.
DR. SEUSS

KEYS FOR LOVING YOUR FAMILY

1. Lead for the benefit of others, not for your own benefit.

2. Be careful in selecting a spouse. It is one of the most important decisions you will ever make.

3. Be present with your family—emotionally and physically.

4. Be careful what you say and do.

5. Honor those in authority over you.

6. If you can't come to grips with your parents and your past, find a professional to walk with you through it.

CHAPTER 5

HOW TO TREAT A WOMAN

I first learned the concept of nonviolence in my marriage.

MOHANDAS GANDHI

THE WAY YOU TREAT WOMEN will impact every other area of your life at some point.

It will stretch beyond your immediate relationship with your wife (or girlfriend) to your friends, parents, and children. Character is revealed in the way you treat others and how you handle these relationships.

Many guys I have known either flex their muscles around women (figuratively, usually) or become completely passive. Neither is the right approach.

Some guys are so bent on being tough—or at least acting tough—that when respect doesn't seem to flow their way naturally, they *demand* it, holding it over everyone around them, including their women. And Christian men are no exception; all too often, we are even worse. Confused by the tension between societal values and what we believe is set out in Scripture, we either fall back on the "head of household" concept as an excuse to take control, or we think Christ requires that we become passive and weak. Because of this, we either reject a real relationship with Jesus or we crumble and abandon our proper roles in our relationships.

The middle road—and the best one to take—is love. According to 1 Corinthians 13, love means doing everything for someone else's benefit. Of course, this *doesn't* mean giving in to that person's every wish or desire, but it does mean making every decision with his or her well-being in mind.

How does this play out in a relationship? There are countless books on how women think, so I'll leave it at this: they are not men. I know that seems obvious, but we can't approach them as we would one of the guys. So how do we show them love? Be involved with them—without bringing our own agendas. Again, do everything for the *benefit* of your loved one. Without being involved—deeply involved—with Lauren for all these years and trying to listen to not only her words but also her heart, I wouldn't have made any progress at all. We've invested time in our marriage. We've talked in the evenings about finances and children. We've gone on dates. And as much as possible, I've tried to create an environment on her terms. The

> **Love means doing everything for someone else's benefit.**

interesting and blessed thing about that is this: she's tried to do the same for me.

The most important way to show love to your girlfriend or wife is to be involved. Listen to her—not to solve the problems of the day, as so often we will try to do. Just listen so she knows you care. She's smart enough to solve her own problems, but she may appreciate your input even more if it's offered at an appropriate time—later. In the meantime, be there for her.

There is a lot of talk in church circles about the role of men and women in marriage. What concerns me is that these discussions tend to focus on who gets to be in charge. But the Bible makes it clear that both husbands and wives are supposed to be looking out for each other's well-being, not concentrating on who has the power. That means, as a husband, I'm supposed to be doing everything for the good of my wife.

You are each gifted differently, and you each have passions—some of which are similar, but many of which are different. The saying that "opposites attract" is not always true in relationships, but I must admit that Lauren and I are as different as night and day in a lot of things. There's a simple explanation for this: we are each uniquely created, like no one else anywhere—no one. And God brought us together to complement each other. Each of us brings what God has created within us to this relationship, for this particular time, for the benefit of each other, our marriage, and all we will impact together through our marriage: children, friends, and others.

Many of you probably aren't married yet. Take your time. Pray that God will show you who your spouse will be. It is one of the most important decisions of your adult life. It will impact everything in your future: your family, your finances, your career, your retirement.

The Bible says in 2 Corinthians 6:14-16 that we are not to be unequally yoked, invoking the metaphor of oxen yoked together to pull a plow. The obvious implication is that if the oxen do not work well together, they won't pull in straight lines and therefore won't be productive. It's an uncomfortable place to be if you're attached at the shoulder.

I think this verse cuts to the heart of the issue: you're to find someone whose basic philosophy of life is the same as yours. In short, is her faith coming from the same source as yours? Are her values?

Beyond that, God has a marvelous ability to complement our lives with partners who can make them that much more complete. That is, I don't think it matters that you see eye to eye on all other issues of the day. I have even heard of instances—albeit rare—in which Colts and Patriots fans have been blissfully married. Anything is possible if *real* love is at the heart of it, and the fabric of our lives often can be richer for it.

CHAPTER 6

FATHERHOOD

One father is more than a hundred schoolmasters.

OLD ENGLISH PROVERB

FATHERHOOD REMAINS ONE OF THE critical foundations for the health of your generation and for those who will follow. The way fatherhood is viewed in the future is in large part dependent upon the way that today's men handle the responsibilities of this role that has been entrusted to them. For this reason, even though most of you are not fathers, I would like to briefly address this topic.

I'm worried about the vacuum we've left in this country with the ever-growing problem of absentee fathers. When the time comes, be there for your children! And not just physically, but emotionally as well. Too many young men and boys are growing up without a male role model to show them what it means to be a man.

Something else to think about is how you speak to your children. What we say is terribly important because children are so emotionally dependent on their fathers. Our words can inspire, rekindle a sense of wonder, and provide direction, or they can dampen spirits, condemn ideas, and destroy initiative. Watch what you say.

Great care should also be taken in what you do. Children are more perceptive than you may think. What you will say as a father is important, but not nearly as much as what you do. They will notice if you are not living consistent with what you're saying and teaching.

But sometimes the best thing you can do as a parent is to be quiet. Our children need to know that we're always there for them, that we're there to help them pick up the pieces of their shattered dreams, to tell them that they're okay, to help them see that failure isn't final, and that when they take their next steps, they will not be alone. Quality time is important, but they need *quantity* time, too, and lots of it. They need to know that we've chosen to be in the room or in the house with them, over all the other interests competing for our time.

> **Fatherhood remains one of the critical foundations for the health of your generation and for those who will follow.**

Fatherhood may seem a long way off, but preparing early will help you meet the challenge as an uncommon man.

CHAPTER 7

RESPECT AUTHORITY

*When I was a boy of fourteen, my father was so
ignorant I could hardly stand to have the old man
around. But when I got to be twenty-one, I was
astonished at how much he had learned in
seven years.*

MARK TWAIN

NOT EVERYTHING MY FATHER DID made
sense to me as a boy—for example, he was a notori-
ous bargain hunger, and we often disagreed on what
was really the best deal. But I learned at an early age
that I should respect him and that I could trust his
authority as my father, whether or not I agreed with
him. His decisions and the consequences he imposed
did not always seem fair to me. But as I got older, it
became increasingly clear that my best interests and
those of my brother and sisters were paramount to
my parents, and they expected us to honor them and
the decisions they made for our lives.

My parents also made it very clear that this was
rooted in God's Word. We were to honor them as the
Bible commanded through our obedience and respect.

I could disagree with them, and often did, but I had to accept their decisions and learn to deal with them.

Parents aren't the only source of authority in our lives. God has placed others over us as well. In Romans 13:1, it says, "Everyone must submit to governing authorities. For all authority comes from God, and those in positions of authority have been placed there by God."

And all of us have positions of authority. We must always be aware of the influence we have on others. Many of us have positions of influence in our school, work, or community activities, or with neighborhood groups, friends, or those we have never even met and perhaps never will. We'll look at your positions of influence in later chapters.

As I mentioned earlier, your parents' authority may not always make sense to you where you are. But be patient with them. They are doing their best. They love you and want what's best for you.

You may have a hard time with honoring your parents and respecting authority. You may not have the benefit of the loving, nurturing, and dedicated parents that I was blessed with.

Maybe you come from a broken home. Maybe you have a parent who left and hasn't come back, leaving a void you still feel today. Maybe you were abused—physically, emotionally, or otherwise—and along with the scars of abuse, there remains a bitterness you can't seem to get beyond. Maybe you don't want to let it go; perhaps you feel that you have the right to be angry for what was done to you. Perhaps you feel it was somehow your fault.

Maybe you view yourself as unworthy, and the hurtful actions of others have colored your idea of what you can expect from your heavenly Father.

You don't want that to be the story for the rest of your life! You may need to seek professional help or talk to a pastor or trusted friend. But somehow you need to get to a place of healing and wholeness. God created you with unique gifts and abilities and a unique purpose. He wants to use you for extraordinary accomplishments.

> **All authority comes from God, and those in positions of authority have been placed there by God.**

The God who created you is still there and loves you with an unconditional and never-ending love. You may have never experienced this kind of unconditional love from your parents. But somehow you need to move on into all the fullness of life that God intended for you. You need to forgive the people who did these things to you. Unresolved bitterness affects *us* more than those we're bitter toward. It ties us down and holds us back from becoming all we were created to be.

God loves you, in spite of the mistakes, failures, and shortcomings in your life. His love is unconditional.

It never ends, and He never leaves. I suspect that may be hard to swallow if the very ones who were supposed to love and protect you were the ones who hurt you the most. But it's true. The God who created you *will never leave you* and *will always love you*.

He stands ready to walk with you for the rest of your life. He will help you draw a line between your past and your future, and He will help you to forgive and move out into all the fullness and freedom of a brand new day. He might even help you get to a place with your parents where you can not only let go of the pain but also begin to honor them by giving them the blessing of your love.

Big step? Huge! But it's possible if you do it with the prayer and help of friends and family who love you now, if you get professional help where needed, and if you lean on the God who will never leave you. Remember: no one will ever love you the way that Jesus loves you. He was with you when you were born, and He is with you now.

PART III

LIFT
YOUR FRIENDS
& OTHERS

Whenever you're in conflict with
someone, there is one factor that
can make the difference between
damaging your relationship and
deepening it. That factor is attitude.
WILLIAM JAMES

KEYS FOR LIFTING YOUR FRIENDS AND OTHERS

1. Choose friends for the sake of friendship, based on values.

2. Listen to the voices of those you trust, not the voices of the crowd.

3. Be open to taking advice from people whose judgment you trust.

4. Conflict can be positive. Don't fear it.

5. Be yourself. Others may need your example, whether you realize it or not.

6. Be intentional about helping others. Give back as you move through life.

CHAPTER 8

FRIENDSHIP

No love, no friendship, can cross the path of our destiny without leaving some mark on it forever.

FRANÇOIS MAURIAC

CHOOSE YOUR FRIENDS FOR THE sake of friendship. It seems like such an obvious statement, but my parents used to say it all the time. Don't choose friends because they are popular, or because they are good-looking, or because they are rich or athletic. Choose your friends because you enjoy them and because they are good people.

Remember, friendship runs two ways. Too often we evaluate a friendship based on the way it benefits *us*. But lasting friendships are formed when we can cause those benefits to flow toward someone else. What benefits do you bring to your friendships?

I'm not sure how well we do with that. We seem so quick to categorize others, so quick to determine people's worth based on what they can do for us, where they live, what they drive or wear, or what their occupation is. It's been my experience that we value NFL coaches far more than we should and nurses and teachers not nearly enough.

Choose your friends for the sake of friendship—their friendship to you, and more importantly, your friendship to them. Start there.

You should also choose your friends based on their values, not their status in society. I saw my folks live out this lesson every day. Within our extended family, I had a number of uncles who worked very different jobs. One was a high-ranking member of law enforcement, another was an autoworker, another was a baker, and so on. It never occurred to me that these positions might carry value; to me, each of them was my uncle. Their value, for me and others who knew them, was not determined by their job titles but by the men they were twenty-four hours a day, whether working, or hanging out at home, or doing something else in their communities.

> **Choose your friends because you enjoy them and because they are good people.**

Similarly, when it came to choosing my friends, my parents encouraged me to hang around people who had inner cores that would build me up. Many of my current friends are coaches. Many are not. I haven't selected any of my friends based on their status. Instead, I look for people of character whose company I enjoy. What I value most about my friends is the way their own life choices reinforce those values that have been ingrained in me for so long by my parents and others.

No doubt if you were asked to do so, you could come up with an exhaustive list of those people in your life that you call friends. But the list would probably become much shorter if you listed the people you seek out when you make your most important decisions. Those whose voices and wisdom you seek when you face a crossroads in your life. Friends who will stand by and guide you when you need it. Friends who put your interests before their own.

Number one on my list of those friends is my bride, Lauren. Hers has been a voice of encouragement, love, character, and godly wisdom for well beyond the years of our marriage. In fact, that is one of the things that attracted me to her. Her voice has always carried messages of importance, pointing me toward what is right and what is in my best interest. Those messages have shaped my character amid the lure and glamour of a world that is constantly trying to make me detour from the path that God has set before me. There are other voices of wisdom in my life as well, friends whose counsel I often seek before making the really important decisions of my life. People who see the same direction for my life that I see—God's direction. I also have friends who will correct me when it's necessary.

Too many of us listen to the voices of the crowd, even when we know better. Often, we do this simply because there are many voices and they are the loudest: the voices of ambition, power, wealth, revenge, greed, pleasure, self-centeredness, and appeasement. At some time in our lives, we have all succumbed to one of those voices. Celebrities, sports figures, and "role models." Church leaders. Married couples. Politicians. Parents. We have all heard them, the voices reflecting the ways of the world.

But even while all those voices bombard us, we need to learn to listen to the quiet voices consistently speaking the truth. These voices come from our parents or our close friends, those people who have been with us in the valleys and on the mountaintops of our journeys. I can still hear some things my mom said forty years ago quite distinctly in my mind today.

And if we listen closely, we may even hear the quiet voice, the whisper, of our God—our dearest friend—pointing us toward the uncommon life that He desires from us.

CHAPTER 9

TAKING COUNSEL

'Tis great confidence in a friend to tell him your faults, greater to tell him his.

BENJAMIN FRANKLIN

I DON'T KNOW EVERYTHING.

There have been enough people in my life through the years who have made that painfully clear to me. Therefore, I must be secure enough to say, "I don't know." In fact, I really need to be secure enough to say, "I have absolutely no idea what you're talking about."

"I don't know" is always a good answer, especially if it is true. "I don't know—could you please enlighten me?" is often an even better answer.

There will always be someone who knows more than you do, which is good. I strongly encourage you to find those people and talk to them. We can learn a lot from people who know more than we do. That's one of the things I really admired about my dad. He talked to everyone—or I should say he *listened* to everyone. Most people described him as quiet, but that's because in most conversations, he listened much more than he talked. He really felt he could learn things from other people.

To me, this is the flip side of mentoring, which we will discuss a bit later. When you are mentoring, you are intentionally reaching out to help someone behind you on the path of life. But when you are seeking counsel, you are looking for someone who is already ahead of you, someone you can learn from. Being open to learning—to being mentored—is necessary for growth but is difficult for some to master. Too often it's a matter of ego or pride, which has a way of hindering our growth and development.

We all know people who lead you to believe they know everything about everything. When I was in college, somebody said, "If after three weeks of class you don't know who the class jerk is, then it's you." Make sure you don't become that person who thinks he has all the answers and isn't open to the counsel of others. I've found that this attitude is often a defense mechanism, masking feelings of insecurity or fear that you'll be exposed for your lack of knowledge.

A good coaching staff is made up of people who are willing to listen to others. If I had all the answers, there would be no point in surrounding myself with bright, creative coaches—and I'm sure the team ownership would be pleased with all the money they would save in salaries. The truth is, though, that we all need to surround ourselves with the very best, smartest, and most trustworthy people we can find. And then we need to turn them loose to do their jobs and offer the input necessary to make us the best we can be.

We all know people who resist change or feel threatened if someone else comes up with an appropriate plan. This kind of person acts as if no idea is a good idea unless it's *his* idea.

Don't be like that. Be open to taking counsel. After all, Proverbs 20:18 tells us that "plans succeed through good counsel; don't go to war [or play a football game!] without wise advice." Instead, surround yourself with the best people you can find and then empower them to do their jobs. Set the vision for the course you want to take. Recognize how significant

> **We can learn a lot from people who know more than we do.**

their differing skills and abilities are to the mission of the cause, team, or organization, and allow them to use those gifts and abilities to get you there. Let them know how important their contributions are to the group's success. Seek their input, listen to them, decide on the direction, and then go there together.

As you do this, conflict is sure to arise. Don't relish conflict, but don't fear it either. Conflict is one of the most misunderstood parts of our existence. It is often unpleasant; many people try to avoid it. Others seem to thrive on the stress of it. I think some even use it to overpower others. Maybe that's why they look for opportunities to bully people.

However, conflict is best seen as an opportunity to understand our differences, since that's when conflict usually arises: when we see something differently.

When a problem does come up, think constructively. You are not attacking the other person, and hopefully he is not attacking you, either. If he is, redirect him to the problem. That is what you both should be focused on: the principle, not the person.

In this day and age, too many people resort to letting arguments become personal—name-calling, mockery, personal attacks. I suppose humans have always done it. We can't stay focused on the matter before us so we get frustrated and lash out; or we realize that our position should change but we aren't confident enough to do so. That seems to be the common approach to conflict.

Don't be like that. Be constructive. Be *uncommon*.

Stay focused on solutions and communication. Admit when you're wrong, but stand your ground when you're right. Sometimes you will have to stand alone, and sometimes for an extended period of time. Other times the mere act of standing for what you believe in will bring others with you, and then you are no longer alone.

Either way, conflict can serve to illuminate truth or illuminate differences. In any event, it doesn't have to be feared.

CHAPTER 10

THE POWER OF POSITIVE INFLUENCE

This above all: to thine own self be true,
And it must follow, as the night the day,
Thou canst not then be false to any man.

WILLIAM SHAKESPEARE'S *HAMLET*, ACT I, SCENE III

PEER PRESSURE WORKS IN BOTH directions. Sometimes we're so busy reacting to peer pressure that we forget we're exerting it on others.

To thine own self be true. Shakespeare wrote this advice four centuries ago, but it's no less true today than it was then, or at any other time in history.

This advice is critically important to remember as you set out in the world. You will come into contact with people who, whether they mean to or not, will exert pressure on you to conform. However, you are also in a position to influence them—for good. You can help your friends make better decisions just by your example. But to be that good example, you must have a clear foundation of who you are.

When I was traded from the Pittsburgh Steelers to the San Francisco 49ers in 1979, many things in my world changed drastically. I went from playing for a Super Bowl–level team in a relatively small, blue-collar city to playing for a very poor team in a large, cosmopolitan area. At twenty-four years old, I was venturing into a different world, one with many more temptations than I had ever experienced before.

Drug use was prevalent there. I wondered how I would respond if someone offered me drugs. I didn't want to look like some small-town kid who had no clue what the "real world" was like. Because of my athletic training, my parents' influence, and my Christian beliefs, I never really considered using drugs. But I did feel out of place, and I sensed that a lot of people were looking at me as being strange.

> **To be a good example, you must have a clear foundation of who you are.**

To thine own self be true.

I later discovered that some guys *were* looking at me. One of my teammates had gotten into the drug culture in San Francisco because he thought that's what pro athletes did. But because I had come from a Super Bowl team in Pittsburgh and I didn't do drugs, it made him feel he didn't have to either. Years later, he told me that my example may have saved his life; it was a lesson in role modeling I've never forgotten.

Becoming a positive role model starts with a look in the mirror. It may take looking back into your life to see things that happened to you for which you are still trying to compensate. Maybe your childhood wasn't all that great. Maybe you failed at things you've tried. Maybe you could have done better in some of the relationships in your life.

But you were created for a reason. It doesn't matter what you missed or how you may have messed up; *your future is still ahead of you*. What will you do with it? What did you learn from past mistakes that might make the journey ahead better? And which of those lessons do you need to model for those around you? Every day we are faced with challenges and the temptation to conform. But God made each of us with unique gifts and characteristics, and being a positive role model starts with being ourselves.

Think for a moment about those relationships in your life that mean the most to you. They probably involve one-on-one time spent face-to-face with each other. Unfortunately, with e-mail, the Internet, texting, and online virtual communities, we may be losing—by our own choices—the opportunities to develop the most meaningful relationships.

Online communities seem to be springing up everywhere, and while having many benefits, they give me cause for concern. I worry that young people may not realize the permanence of posting things online or see the danger in making themselves so vulnerable and accessible to strangers.

My biggest concern, however, is that in forming

virtual bonds, we may be forsaking true human interaction. As we interact via bits and bytes, we run the risk of further isolating ourselves. Gone are the days of neighborhoods with front porches and kids riding their bikes to a friend's house. Now cars pull into garages and the doors close behind them.

Life was meant to be lived in community. We learn from others what it means to be a man and what it means to be part of a group. I don't mind these technological advances, but let me add a word of caution: give careful thought to your use of them. We are always connected these days, via cell phones, the Internet, or other electronic devices. That's great. But I think we need to make sure we're not so connected with *everything* out there that we miss the chance to be quiet and connect with the people directly in front of us. Because it's in those real-life connections that the power of our personal influence can have life-changing, long-lasting impact.

No matter where you are in your life's journey, you can begin today to be intentional about leaving a trail of positive memories in the lives of those around you. Memories they will cling to in the rough spots they face over the course of their lives. Memories that will draw them closer to you and affirm their value to you and to themselves.

CHAPTER 11

MENTORING

The light which experience gives is a lantern on the stern, which shines only on the waves behind us.

SAMUEL TAYLOR COLERIDGE

ISAAC NEWTON WROTE, "IF I have seen further it is by standing upon the shoulders of giants." Newton was referring to those people who look out for our best interests and help us become all we were intended to be. True giants have proven that they are wise, experienced, and loyal—strong enough to hold us on their shoulders.

At its essence, that is what mentoring is: building character into the lives of others and leaving a legacy.

Of all the great people I've had the privilege of coaching, Derrick Brooks is one of my favorites. Not only is he a great player, but he has also always been concerned with giving back.

After he arrived in Tampa in 1995, Derrick started hanging out at a local Boys & Girls Club. Derrick initially anticipated starting a ticket program to help kids attend our games, but he wanted to do more than that. He was looking to build into their lives.

His idea was to take the kids on a fun but inspiring trip. Derrick developed a yearlong curriculum in which the kids chose a place they would like to visit and then spent a year learning about their destination. Derrick was amazed by the number of kids who had never been outside of Tampa, and he committed himself to broadening their horizons and motivating them to think of themselves as future leaders who could make a difference in their world.

That is mentoring. That is leaving a legacy. Last year, the first wave of the "Brooks Bunch" graduated from college, and there's no doubt in my mind that Derrick's involvement in their lives played a big part in many of those kids' successes.

That is what mentoring is: building character into the lives of others and leaving a legacy.

Not everyone has the financial means to take students on trips. But I don't believe that's the most important part of what he's done. Mentoring takes more than just money. It takes time. It requires the sacrifice of other things you could be doing.

Look outside of yourself for someone you can reach out to. Guys younger than you need mentors, and you can be one, with whatever gifts and experiences you bring. Trust me: there is a child out there who needs to know that you care.

PART IV

REACH
YOUR FULL
POTENTIAL

Don't think you're on the
right road just because
it's a well-beaten path.
AUTHOR UNKNOWN

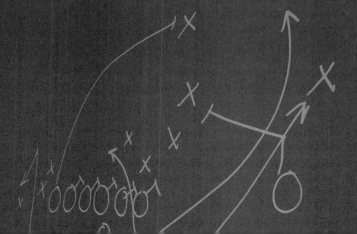

KEYS FOR REACHING YOUR FULL POTENTIAL

1. Be positive. Your mind is more powerful than you think.

2. Your education matters. Sports are great . . . as a complement to academics.

3. Find employment that excites you for reasons beyond the salary.

4. Make conservative decisions with debt.

5. Goals are important, but make sure they are worthy goals—you just might reach them!

6. Be careful with mind-altering substances, even legal ones. Addiction can sneak up and destroy your life.

7. You will fail. Remember that, but don't fear it.

CHAPTER 12

POWERFUL THOUGHTS

What I always feared has happened to me.
What I dreaded has come true.

JOB 3:25

LIFE IS CHALLENGING. I WISH I could tell you that you'll always be on top of the mountain, but the reality is that there are days when nothing will go right, when not only will you not be on top, you may not even be able to figure out which way is up. Do yourself a favor, and don't make it any harder than it has to be. In those moments, be careful how you speak to, think of, conduct, and develop yourself.

We have an amazing ability to accomplish whatever our minds tell us we can do. The great American novelist Henry James directed, "Believe that life is worth living, and your belief will help create the fact." James could have been a football coach. The first thing you have to do when you're trying to turn a football franchise from a loser to a winner is create the *belief* that you can win. Most of the time the talent is already there to accomplish great things, but there is no belief that it will happen.

Our minds are powerful instruments and should not be taken lightly. I have heard about prisoners of war who were able to play golf or perform other skills they didn't have prior to their solitary confinement. While they had been held captive, they had merely visualized what they wanted to accomplish.

All football teams rely on visualization to increase their chances of success. That's what we work on in practice. We run the plays we will use in the game and fine-tune them against our "look squad." The look squad consists of our backup players, whose function is to simulate the other team's techniques so our first-team players see exactly how our plays will work during a game. By running a play several times during the week, and seeing it successfully executed, we can visualize exactly how it's going to look on Sunday. If we've been sharp in practice, then we have confidence that it will go the same way during the game.

Being disciplined in your approach to each day and accomplishing the things you dream of starts by disciplining your thoughts. I'm not suggesting that life will be easy or blessings will be showered upon you if you start thinking positively; but I am suggesting that negative thinking can't help but set you back.

Bill Russell, an NBA all-star for years with the Boston Celtics and one of the all-time greatest winners in any sport, understood the importance of positive as well as negative thinking. "The idea is not to block every shot. The idea is to make your opponent believe that you might block every shot," he said. If the opponent was afraid of having his shot blocked, Russell knew he didn't have to always try to block it. Instead of focusing on putting the ball into the basket, the opponent would shift his eye contact from his goal to Russell and eventually miss shots because he was certain that Russell could be everywhere at once. He couldn't, of course, but a little doubt can do a lot of damage, especially if it becomes the focus of your thoughts.

Whatever we think will often be the outcome of any given situation. I'm inclined to think there is an actual law of self-fulfilling prophecies. I have watched many teams take the field feeling it wasn't their day, only to find out at the end of the game that it wasn't. I have also been a part of many more teams that have headed out of the locker room expect-

> **Whatever we think will often be the outcome of any given situation.**

ing to execute every play and come out victorious at the end of the game. And they did. Sure, preparation and talent go a long way toward creating that positive belief—but more often than not, it's the expectation of success that defines championship teams.

Building expectations is something we all have to do. You won't always rise to the level of the expectations you have for yourself, but you will never be able to rise above the imaginary ceiling you construct in your mind. How high do you want to set those expectations? How high would you like to go?

Your life will also be affected by how much you allow the things around you to affect the direction of your journey. You will not be able to do anything about removing all the distractions you find along the way. The key is to continue to focus your thoughts on where you want to go, regardless of those distractions.

My friend Ken Whitten says, "What's down in the well will come up in the bucket." What is down in your well? From what source does the water in your well come? From where do you draw strength and direction for your life?

The writer of Hebrews recounted incident after incident of saints who had demonstrated that the source of their strength came from God, even without being able to see the end of the journey He had set out for them. They imagined and believed in a future painted by the hand of the One who had proven His faithfulness to them time and time again. Their lives and hearts—and their visions for their futures—were shaped by their faith in God and by the vision He had set before them.

What's down in your well? Whatever is there will govern the thoughts for your today and your tomorrow. Fill it well.

CHAPTER 13

EDUCATION AND ATHLETICS

"Son, looks to me like you're spending too much time on one subject."

SHELBY METCALF, TEXAS A&M BASKETBALL COACH, TO A PLAYER WHO RECEIVED ONE D AND FOUR FS

IF THERE WERE EVER AREAS in which we seem to have switched the price tags, it's in the areas of education and athletics. Our society places great weight on athletic achievement. (The irony that you're reading this book, written by a sports figure, is not lost on me.) Yet in your most rational moments, in thinking through the full implications of, for instance, life in the NFL—a profession with an average career of 3.3 years, in which the possibility of permanent physical injury is always present, that offers limited and under-developed skills off the athletic field, and is marked by broken marriages and dysfunctional families—would you really choose that over a future that could make you happy and able to contribute to society? We shouldn't, but sadly, many of us do.

We see it again and again. We see it when children

are encouraged or, worse, pushed to compete in sports. We see it in the overzealous Little League parents. We see it when parents and coaches try to live vicariously through their children's athletic achievements. The cold, hard facts are that far less than one percent—more like one-tenth of one percent—of high school athletes will grow up to be professional athletes. You can only imagine how small that percentage might be for Little Leaguers.

In the meantime, those children are often not encouraged to spend the same time and attention obtaining a full and complete education, even though the odds are that high school athletes will need to use that education in their lives more than their athletic training. Even for the players who do make it to the NFL and are making more money than most people their age, those post-career skills are crucial. Given that average career of 3.3 years, most guys will be around twenty-six years old when that big money stops coming in, and they'll still have most of their adult lives ahead of them. As they look for work, they begin to understand that in this new job market, athletic skills don't count for much. And all too often, their nonathletic skills have never been nurtured.

The other side effect of this focus on athletic achievement is that the true meaning has often been lost. Sports should be about enjoyment, cooperation, team building, learning to deal with adversity, building character, and pursuing excellence. But those days are going the way of eight-track tapes and twelve-inch televisions.

I'm grateful that my parents supported my siblings and me in our involvement in sports and other activities, but they also wanted us to be well-rounded. Somehow I was one of the one-tenth of one percent—I did have the opportunity to play professional sports—although after three years in the NFL, I still needed other life skills to support myself as a twenty-five-year-old whose athletic career was over.

One of the best examples to me in the area of education and athletics was Ernest Cook. I met him when I was a high school senior, during my recruiting trip to the University of Minnesota. He had finished his playing days the year before. He was drafted by an NFL club but didn't sign, choosing instead to attend medical school.

> Odds are that high school athletes will need to use education in their lives more than their athletic training.

The coaches and administrators at every school I visited gave a standard spiel to high school recruits about the education they were offering, but talking to Ernie was completely different from what I had heard from everybody else. Since I had grown up with educators for parents, his message that weekend resonated with me, so much that I still remember much of it today.

"They told me that I could go to the NFL, but I never cared about that," he told me. "Football was just a chance to get a scholarship, and the coaches here told me that they'd help me get into medical school, which they did." I asked him why he chose not to try pro football, even though he had been drafted. I didn't know anyone at the time who wouldn't try to play if they had the chance. Ernie told me, however, that his goal had never been to play pro football. It had always been to become a doctor. I was impressed and somewhat shocked by that—a talented athlete, one of the university's star players, who wasn't all hyped up to play pro football and wasn't looking for the money, fame, and notoriety that went along with the NFL. Ernest wanted an uncommon route through the adventure of life.

Ernie Cook inspired me to do well in school because he took the right approach to being a student-athlete. He went against the peer pressure of the environment.

Booker T. Washington once said, "If you can't read, it's going to be hard to realize dreams." Most of us can read, but do we have the other skills necessary for fulfilling all that we were designed to be? Make sure that you do everything in your power to give yourself that chance so that you will not live your life with your talents untapped.

CHAPTER 14

CAREER, WORK, AND MONEY

The mercenaries will always beat the draftees, but the volunteers will crush them both.

CHUCK NOLL

I'VE SEEN IT TIME AND again: high school and college students trying to figure out what they are going to do—and why. Ultimately, it's not really a career question. It's a purpose question. *What am I going to do with my life?* We all need to answer the deep questions of purpose, meaning, and fulfillment in life.

Rather than making choices on the basis of money, however, select something *that you want to do*. It's great to love your work, and a blessing to enjoy it.

As the head coach of the Pittsburgh Steelers, Coach Noll was concerned not only for our physical well-being but also for the emotional health of the team. He loved the quote at the beginning of this chapter. People forced into something will be least effective, while those with external motivation (money, in the case of the mercenaries) will be effective to a point. However, those with internal drive, who have signed on because their *hearts* are in it, will rise to the top. Money may get you started, but it won't be enough to sustain you when the times become difficult.

Coach Noll told me repeatedly that I should "never make a job decision based on money"—first when I was a player, then when I was one of his coaches. He wasn't disparaging money or its ability to allow you to do things in life, but rather making sure that I understood its limitations.

It's easy to compare dollars to dollars, and when we have the opportunity to earn more, it's tempting to think, *This is best for me*, or *That employer values me more*, or *That company respects me more*. The reality is, however, money isn't really a good measure of what's best for you. And the more you base critical decisions on monetary evidence, the more those around you will come to believe that money is the most important thing in your life.

> **Money isn't really a good measure of what's best for you.**

I also have to say this: poor money decisions can tie your hands, reduce your options, and cause you to make bad decisions out of desperation. Credit card companies spend hundreds of millions of dollars to market their cards to students and young people—and they aren't spending those amounts to do you a favor. Borrowing money is expensive. That's not something the credit card companies will tell you. It's lucrative for those companies to get you to spend beyond your means, buying stuff you don't need with money you don't have. Once they get their hooks in you, it is very difficult to dig your way out. Don't do it.

You may not find that career path that gets you excited right away. Keep looking, but give your current position a chance. Many entry- and intermediate-level positions are not terribly exciting, but they may be important stepping-stones along the way. The position might involve the development of skills that feel tedious or "beneath you," but all jobs are really training for subsequent ones. Sometimes employers use entry-level positions to evaluate an employee's abilities and commitment. Many positions require trust, and employers need to know they can trust you with little things that seem menial before they will trust you with more. Be careful that you aren't evaluating a position on the wrong scale.

At the same time, keep in mind that you don't have to do it forever. Too many people decide that they'll find their "it" later, whatever *it* is they were meant to do professionally, or maybe whatever *it* means in terms of getting them involved in the community. Too many people defer their lives until they arrive somewhere and never truly live. Make sure that's not you.

Many of us walk in the door at the end of the day carrying our frustrations with us. When we lose a game on a last-second field goal, it's tough for me to really be excited about playing Candy Land with the kids. But I have to make myself do it. Whether it's your family or friends—or your blood pressure—no one deserves to be saddled with whatever happened at the office. Tomorrow will have enough problems of its own. Don't start worrying about them now. Don't let the emotion of the day govern your home life and free time.

Some people use work as an escape from their home lives, simply ignoring anything that doesn't have to do with their careers. Your work may be like that, too. There's always more preparation, more research, more to do to get ahead. But at some point I think we have to be willing to stand behind what we've done. When you've given a solid day's work, that should be enough.

And when you get home, be home. Your mind will no doubt wander to your work, but try to keep that to a minimum. The people you love and who love you deserve quality, fully committed time. Others know when you're there simply as a warm body but otherwise a thousand miles away. You have to make a conscious effort not to do that.

Make sure that you're not so busy making a living that you forget to actually *live*.

CHAPTER 15

GOALS AND RISK

Avoiding danger is no safer in the long run than outright exposure. Life is either a daring adventure or nothing.

HELEN KELLER

MATT EMMONS IS A WORLD-CHAMPION marksman. In the 2004 Summer Olympics, he had a significant lead when he entered the final round of competition. He hit the bull's-eye on his three shots, then looked on, puzzled, as the automatic scoring system did not credit his shots. It was untouched. No holes.

The target in the next lane, however, had three extra holes. His mistake cost him, and he finished eighth. This story illustrates that without a goal—your *own* goal—you won't reach all that you're capable of. Unless you are focused on the passions of your heart and are striving toward them, you won't achieve all that God has in store for you.

My goals are usually qualitative rather than quantitative. I aim for a team that is as good as it can be and guys who are an asset to the community and good role models. Those are the things I reflect on at the end of each year as I analyze our season. I measure our teams by how we performed compared to our potential—that's really the only reasonable measurement to use.

As for me, I try to improve each year. When I was a young assistant, my goal was to learn enough to be a good defensive coach and to help my players play as well as possible. Later, it was to continue to improve, so that I might merit consideration as a defensive coordinator. Still later, it was to put myself in a position to become a head coach.

Take note, however. Though I wanted to be a coordinator and head coach, I continued to focus on a goal that was within my control: to hone my coaching abilities in order to be ready for those positions. I couldn't control whether or not I was hired. Some things are up to others—and God—and therefore aren't realistic to hold over yourself.

Sometimes goals require risk. The old saying that "you can't steal second with your foot still on first" is true not only in baseball but also in life. When Herm Edwards left my staff in Tampa Bay to become the head coach of the New York Jets, I was forced to replace a terrific coach. I hired Mike Tomlin, a young coach out of the University of Cincinnati. Mike had been at the university for only two years, but I hired him because I loved what I saw: a teacher with a high energy level. Some people may have thought I was taking a chance to hire someone with no NFL experience.

But Mike was the one who took a bigger risk. He had been secure in his position in Cincinnati. Yet he joined a staff in transition, a club where rumors were circulating whether any of us would keep our jobs if we didn't go to the Super Bowl. Mike could have very easily been out of a job the following season. Though many would think that coming to the Buccaneers from the University of Cincinnati was a no-brainer, Mike had to consider his options.

> One great life lesson I've learned from sports is that no one wins every game.

His risk paid off. I was fired after that season, but Mike stayed with Tampa. Seven years after his decision not to play it safe, Mike was named the head coach of the Pittsburgh Steelers.

Sometimes, taking a risk doesn't necessarily pay off. When it was time for me to leave the Steelers in 1988, I was offered jobs with two coaches who ended up in the Hall of Fame, both in the same off-season: Bill Parcells of the New York Giants and Bill Walsh of the San Francisco 49ers. I also had good interviews with coaches in Cincinnati and Kansas City. All four men were great coaches and good people.

However, Lauren and I were starting a family, and we decided that New York and San Francisco were more than we wanted to undertake. I didn't get offered the job in Cincinnati, so we ended up in Kansas City.

The quality of life in Kansas City was great, and it was a perfect place to start raising children. But after three years with the Chiefs, I needed to move on. In the meantime, the Giants and the 49ers had each won a Super Bowl. It would have been easy to second-guess my decision, but there really is no safe path through life.

What I've learned is to gather as much information as possible at the time, pray about things, make a decision, and move on. I try to learn from my decisions and the consequences so I don't repeat mistakes, but I don't second-guess choices I've already made.

Unless you get a chance to undo those decisions, it's best to press on and give yourself a break, while doing the best you can with where you are. One great life lesson I've learned from sports is that no one wins every game. And we *can* win championships even after losing some games.

Sometimes others will second-guess your decisions, especially if they don't share your values. Many people believe that you should never pass up advancement at work. If you pass up a promotion—or quit a position—because you are not involved enough at home, or because you are in a location that isn't conducive to raising children, the critics will suggest that you're being irresponsible.

Don't listen to them. Have the courage of your convictions. Be uncommon.

CHAPTER 16

ALCOHOL AND DRUGS

Drunkenness is simply voluntary insanity.

SENECA

IN APRIL 2001, A GROUP of us were gathered in Jerry Angelo's office at our team headquarters, having just completed what would be my final draft with the Buccaneers. We were chatting about the completed draft and other topics. The offices were snug, and the six of us were seated on extra chairs or any available surface. Shortly after 10:00, I headed home.

My coauthor, Nathan, who was part of the Bucs' scouting department at the time, was also in the room, and as soon as the door closed behind me, he was ordered to his feet.

As he stood, he realized the towel he had been sitting on was covering the beer cooler. Out of respect for me, they had waited until I was gone.

I had tried to tell those guys for years that even though I don't drink, I didn't mind if they did. I don't mind parties—Jesus went to plenty of parties. And just because drinking isn't the right choice for me, it doesn't mean that others can't partake; after all, Jesus' first miracle was turning water into wine. Even so, for whatever reason, they wouldn't drink around me.

As I said, I don't have a problem with anyone having a drink. What I do mind is our society's inability to see alcohol for what it is: a drug. We have strongly warned children about tobacco and illegal drugs, but I am concerned about what sometimes seems to be a "look the other way" relationship with alcohol. And the example this sets for our young people is particularly disturbing. We don't allow anyone to drink who is under the age of twenty-one, which I completely agree with. The unintended consequence of that law, however, is unfortunate. Because they can't legally drink until twenty-one, many young men now view that twenty-first birthday drink as a rite of passage into manhood. The law seems to have made drinking more attractive because it is forbidden until then.

Be careful with alcohol, and don't get near anything else that's mind-altering.

As I have reflected on my father's influence in my life, one of the things I am most grateful for is that he chose not to drink any alcohol. It would have been fine if he did, but his abstinence was a powerful example for me, maybe even more than he might have realized at the time. Whether in high school or college, whenever I found myself in a situation in which everybody was drinking, I always thought of my dad. Because someone that I respected so highly had chosen to not drink, I could make the same choice with confidence.

In addition to my dad, I also benefited from positive peer pressure. On the flight home after my first road game as a member of the Steelers, I saw that the flight attendants were passing out beer. I didn't drink, but as the new guy on the team, I was still a little nervous, not sure what to do.

Then I noticed some of the guys were giving the beers back or giving them away, so I did the same. It was a moment of positive peer pressure for me. Their example on that plane ride home helped me to stay strong in my decision.

As for any other mind-altering substances, my advice is simple: just don't bother. The upside is so limited and fleeting—a chance for escape, I suppose—but the downside, coming either from one bad decision or a lifetime of addiction struggles, is not worth it.

We had a player with the Colts who had worked his way from being an undrafted player out of college to being a starter for our team. All that changed when he was stopped for a speeding violation. The officer noticed a smell of marijuana in the car and found some in the vehicle. The player was arrested, and by the end of the next day, he was no longer a Colt. This player knew our organization's stance on drugs. The whole course of his professional career changed in one moment. But that's nothing compared to Len Bias. After being an NBA first-round pick in 1986, Bias's life ended at twenty-two as the result of a cocaine overdose. Eight days after Bias's death, twenty-three-year-old Don Rogers, a Pro Bowl free safety for the Cleveland Browns, died the same way at his bachelor party the night before he was to be married.

Every day, young people die as a result of alcohol and drug abuse. They're usually not as high profile as these two young men, but their deaths are just as tragic. Because I've never used drugs, I don't know how good they can temporarily make you feel. But no matter how good it is, I simply can't believe it could be worth the risk.

I know there are many people who can "drink responsibly," as the commercials urge us to do. But can you really be sure? How do you know that you'll be able to remain in control? How do you know you won't have one too many? Are you sure you won't become addicted?

Be careful with alcohol, and don't get near anything else that's mind-altering. It's just not worth being part of the crowd in that way, and the downside may be far worse than the upside could ever be.

CHAPTER 17

FAILURE

Only those who dare to fail greatly can ever achieve greatly.

ROBERT F. KENNEDY

I'M OFTEN INTRODUCED AS ONE of only three people to win a Super Bowl as a player and as a head coach. What they don't always say is that there were twenty-seven straight seasons that ended in disappointment between those two Super Bowl wins.

What I've learned through a life in sports is that failure happens regularly. And failure, as it turns out, is a constant in the human experience. I hope that you will fail less than I have, but we all fail. Count on it. The more I learned about those people I admired for their successes, the more I also began to admire them for how they handled failures. Success is really a journey of persistence and perseverance in spite of failure.

The difference between failure and adversity, I suppose, is that failure is viewed as a result, while adversity is seen as something you work your way through. To accomplish your goals, however, I think failure has to be viewed as part of the process. Thomas

Edison said that he didn't fail repeatedly; he merely found ten thousand ways *not* to make a lightbulb.

The journey through adversity is inevitable if we're striving for improvement. If things progress smoothly, where's the need for self-examination and growth? Through pressure, stress, and adversity, we are strengthened—in our character, in our faith, and in our ability to get out of bed again and give it one more try.

> **Success is really a journey of persistence and perseverance in spite of failure.**

Our players often talk about being "tough," but I'm not sure they grasp what that means. Toughness is shown in how you respond to adversity. We don't always get a happy ending, and sometimes the middle isn't so happy either. You never really know how tough people are until they encounter the rough spots.

The truly tough man is the one who stays grounded in his values and focused on his goals when things are challenging. When things don't go according to plan, the tough man will exhibit a determination to reach his goal no matter the obstacles.

People often ask the question, "Why does God allow bad things to happen to good people?" Obviously, there are no easy answers. But I do know this: God is constantly working in us through it all, molding and shaping us into what He created us to be, and it's in the valleys of our failures where He is working the hardest, making us into something uncommon.

PART V

ESTABLISH A
MISSION
THAT MATTERS

Your life is an occasion.
Rise to it.
*MR. MAGORIUM'S
WONDER EMPORIUM*

KEYS FOR ESTABLISHING A MISSION THAT MATTERS

1. Be aware that the world emphasizes style, but substance is what really matters.

2. Make a conscious decision to determine your priorities. Be prepared to start making your actions complement your list of priorities.

3. Never confuse what you do with who you are.

4. Follow your dreams. Don't take them to your grave.

5. Learn to discipline yourself so that you can begin to enjoy more of life the way you want to enjoy it.

CHAPTER 18

STYLE VERSUS SUBSTANCE

Don't settle for style. Succeed in substance.

WYNTON MARSALIS

I HAVE A VIVID RECOLLECTION of eighth grade—1968—and wanting a pair of Chuck Taylor basketball shoes. Everybody had a pair. They were Converse's most popular shoe, a canvas high-top. It's hard to imagine today, but back then . . . wow.

My father took me to the store for new shoes. The Chuck Taylors were $7.99. My dad thought I should get the Kmart version, which were $3.99. I was distressed.

My dad showed me that Kmart's store brand and the Converse shoes were made of the same material, with the same quality, and that the price difference was due to all the marketing hype. I tried to explain how important it was to have the cool shoes and how I didn't want to stand out by wearing the Kmart ones.

My dad didn't say that I couldn't get the shoes; he just said that *he* wouldn't spend the extra money to buy them. His obligation was to provide me with safe, comfortable equipment for my activities. If I wanted to go beyond that, it was up to me. I remember what he said that day: "They are identical, but if it matters enough to you, then you can earn the four dollars to pay the difference." It was my first lesson in style versus substance.

I chose the Chuck Taylors, understanding that I was choosing style. And I worked extra jobs beyond my regular chores for a month to pay off the four dollars my dad had advanced me to buy the shoes.

The battle between style and substance happens in football a lot, just as it does in life. Fans and the media perceive certain players as different people than the ones their families and friends know. They look at certain teams in ways that may not be accurate. Analysts are always using terms like "a finesse team, a physical team, a dome team, an offensive team," and so on.

But to win and be effective, I want our players to know what they're really dealing with, so we try to dig beyond the perception and look at the reality. Perceptions are built by a lot of things: reputations, media portrayals, sometimes even past performance. Uncovering reality sometimes requires a little work.

The first step in developing a good game plan is to determine who we really are—or should be—beyond the world's perceptions and beyond the lure of who society says we should be. It's important to know exactly who you are, both individually and as a team. You need to know your strengths and weaknesses, as well as those of your opponent. That's also a good first step in developing a solid game plan for becoming an uncommon man.

There are a lot of perceptions today about manhood, masculinity, and how to succeed in this world. I think we have to look deeper into things and use resources like the Bible to help us define what manhood truly is.

One of the most compelling and distorted perceptions is that respect comes from status. We tend to focus on what we do, how much we earn, what we look like, what we wear, and what we have. Therefore, it becomes important to us to have a job that will provide the type of status we want, as well as enough income to be able to buy the stuff that will add to that status. The media equates all these things with a certain level of respect. We see it played up in magazines, television shows, and movies. Such a constant onslaught perpetuates the perception that respect comes from status.

> It's important to know exactly who you are, both individually and as a team.

And then we begin to view and evaluate other people that way as well. If they don't have certain types of jobs, if they don't dress a certain way, if they don't have money or the material things that we equate with a certain level of status, we decide that they probably aren't successful and don't have significance, and we don't respect them.

With this mind-set, status becomes one of the most important measures of a man's masculinity. It's style over substance, perception over reality—everywhere you look. Success, or at least the appearance of success, becomes more important than anything else. And we allow our feelings of personal significance and worth to be shaped by it. I think that's why so many guys have trouble when they leave football. They don't feel they have the status they once enjoyed, so it's hard for them to find significance in anything else. Of course, this quest for significance plagues men in all walks of life, not just in football.

Many young men are really into the kind of car they drive and the brand of clothes they wear. Again, it's the idea that we somehow derive status from these things, with style being the key. Somewhere we've lost the concept that respect comes from appreciating who a person is inside and what he is truly all about.

The real danger here is that choosing style over substance keeps us from valuing those things that truly do have worth. Being loyal to your family, modeling proper behavior for others, mentoring the less fortunate—these things may not give us status in today's world, but they are important to God.

Substance or style—the choice is clear if we want to live the significant lives we were meant to live.

CHAPTER 19

PRIORITIES

If people concentrated on the really important things in life, there'd be a shortage of fishing poles.

DOUG LARSON

NOWHERE IN OUR LIVES IS the tension greater than in the area of setting the priorities that matter most. And nothing is tougher than looking in the mirror and seeing all the mistakes we've made. Yet the complete story of our lives is not fully written; change is still possible, and we can still take control of our priorities.

Near the end of his life, Solomon, the king of Israel and a man with power, intelligence, talents, pleasures, and riches beyond compare, put it this way: "What do people get for all their hard work under the sun? . . . I observed everything going on under the sun, and really, it is all meaningless—like chasing the wind" (Ecclesiastes 1:3, 14).

Solomon says that to live a life seeking worldly things is like "chasing the wind." He clearly tells us, from his own experience, that life rooted solely in worldly values and riches is "completely meaning-less." It is empty and will not satisfy.

And at the end of his life, after all of his experiences, Solomon wrote, "Don't let the excitement of youth cause you to forget your Creator. Honor him in your youth before you grow old. . . . Fear God and obey his commands, for this is everyone's duty" (Ecclesiastes 12:1, 13). Solomon's answer to a meaningful, fulfilling life is God.

Too many men I have known live lives seeking fame, fortune, recognition and rewards, comfort and material things, and financial security. Their priorities begin there, and—since those things don't tend to leave time for anything else—they usually end there.

Yet on their deathbeds, these men wouldn't ask their bankers to come to their bedside. No, all of a sudden those things don't seem to matter. At the end of their lives, these men ask for their families and others who are important to them. Sadly, the people who have been there all along were not a high prior-ity to them when they were healthy.

In the last ten years, I have lost my mother, my father, and my oldest son. As a result of my son's death, I've talked to hundreds of parents who have also lost children and to hundreds of kids who have lost sib-lings. Everyone I speak with feels just as I do: when you lose loved ones, no matter how old they are, you always wish you had more time to spend with them. I spent forty-six years with my mom, forty-eight with my dad, and eighteen with my son. I am grateful for the memories I have, but I still wish there had been more. But *we never know for sure how long God will give us with the people we love.* It doesn't always seem fair, but I think God uses those times to remind us not to take life and love for granted. He wants us to keep our priorities in order. I told our players all the time that even though we put a lot of time and hard work into preparing for games, they should never let their work come before their families. If they do, I know someday they'll regret it.

The sad truth is that for too many of us, this is the story of our lives. But it doesn't have to be. Yes, shifting your priorities will require some changes in your life, but in the end it will be more than worth it.

Making a change begins with the principles that Solomon learned late in his life. A life centered on Christ, one that "chases after God," will not only help to free us from being preoccupied with our success, our careers, and our finances—all of which Solomon says is "chasing the wind"—but it also will redirect our focus so that we can learn to embrace the priorities that truly matter.

Coach Tom Landry pointed out that before he began to follow Christ, football was his number-one priority. His wife and family were somewhere down the list, though he was not sure where. However, after he began to walk in a personal relationship with Jesus Christ, he redefined his priorities. Next to his relationship with Christ, his family became most important. He continued to excel in coaching football, but it was no longer his number-one priority. He made sure that it was always below the priorities of his faith and his family.

We have all missed too many memories and moments in our lives because of poorly ordered priorities. But even so, it's never too late to set things straight and begin to enjoy God's blessings that are all around us.

Solomon's answer to a meaningful, fulfilling life is God.

So how do you begin to set the right priorities for your life against the pull of the things the world says are important? It's not easy, but it's absolutely essential if you want to make sure you don't miss the things that matter most.

Start here: "Seek first [God's] kingdom and his righteousness" (Matthew 6:33, NIV). Take a few moments to be quiet and spend time with God. He will lessen your worries about tomorrow and release you from the breathless pace of the world's "urgent" priorities.

Dedicating a few hours of your time to the priorities God has entrusted to you may not seem significant right now, but *to those who need you*, it could make all the difference in their lives, and in yours.

CHAPTER 20

BEING VERSUS DOING

Insist upon yourself. Be original.

RALPH WALDO EMERSON

IN OUR SOCIETY, THE STRUGGLE between *being* and *doing* starts early and is often innocently encouraged. Children are asked what they want to be when they grow up, which really means what they want to *do*.

Some children aspire to be bankers, or professional athletes, or the next American Idol, or an Olympic gold-medal winner. Maybe they want to make lots of money, live in a big house, or have many cars. Great dreams—but they are all related to *doing*, not *being*. Those dreams tell us nothing about who children are, or want to be, inside—what their values and priorities are—those things that will guide them through all the things they will *do*.

I believe we all struggle with this, but it seems it may even be a greater challenge for men. Men feel pressured to tie their personal value to their career. Too often we believe a man's value is determined solely by his achievements and measured against the standards of a world that pays homage to winning.

Unfortunately, many players feel this pressure, deriving their value from what they do and accomplish. They confuse what they do for a living with who they are inside. Once they're done with football, they aren't sure who they are.

A negative job review or getting fired can be devastating. Though it is understandably traumatic, it doesn't have to be defining. I hope you'll never go through it. But if you do, take a step back and remember that your career is not you. It should not, and does not, define *who you are as a person*.

> **Remember that your career is not you. It should not, and does not, define *who you are as a person.***

Every day in my line of work, I receive performance evaluations, often by people unqualified to give them. I decided long ago that I would analyze the criticisms for things that might be helpful. I also realize that I can't control what is said, and I will not let harsh criticism affect my sense of who I am. I know that God created me with all of my strengths and limitations. Somebody pointing out the limitations, real or otherwise, doesn't change my strengths or that I am and will always remain a child of God.

Being versus doing—distinguishing between them will make all the difference in the lives we live.

CHAPTER 21

FOLLOWING YOUR DREAMS

Life's like a movie, write your own ending.

THE MUPPET MOVIE

I ONCE READ AN ARTICLE about Michael Westbrook. Westbrook was a wide receiver from the University of Colorado, drafted as the fourth overall pick by the Washington Redskins in 1995. The interesting thing about the article was learning about how much he *disliked* football. He didn't like the violence of the game, the phony nature he perceived from the players, the pressure from the coaches and fans. He said he continued to play because he was trying to please others and didn't give much thought about doing what pleased him.

A great deal of this book touches on relationships. Others matter, and putting them first is often a critical part of being an uncommon man. But Westbrook's story illustrates an important point.

God placed certain things in your heart. He gave you passions that others don't have. Society may not value those things as much as you do, and people may try to push you into a career that pleases their desires, but at some point, you need to answer the call that God has placed upon you and you alone. You have gifts, abilities, and dreams that no one else has. The things that excite you may not excite me, and that's great. Together we make up the tapestry of humanity. Just make sure that you follow the dreams God placed within *your* heart so that together we can create something beautiful.

I wrote a children's book in which I told the story of my younger brother, Linden. Linden was a bright kid but had trouble committing himself to academics—he preferred to make his classmates laugh. He also felt pressure because people were telling him that he needed to follow me into athletics. I think he enjoyed sports, but he wasn't excited about them the way I was. Finally, he was able to focus on something he wanted to do: dentistry. He was an above-average student in high school, but he blossomed into an outstanding student at Grand Valley State and then in dental school at the University of Minnesota—once he had a dream to pursue. He had finally connected with the passion that God had placed within his heart.

Our children love *The Muppet Movie*, which is all about integrity—the integrity of Kermit the frog. He leaves the swamp to go to Hollywood at the urging of a talent agent, who promises he can become rich and famous. So Kermit sets his face toward Hollywood, not to be rich and famous but to follow his dream to "make millions happy." He makes a promise to himself and to the dream. The movie is the story of his journey to fulfill that promise.

At every turn along the way, he is approached by Doc Hopper, an entrepreneur seeking a "spokesfrog" for his chain of frog leg restaurants. Each time, Kermit refuses the offer of easy wealth, intent on fulfilling his dream.

At a critical juncture of the film, their broken-down Studebaker has caused Kermit and all who have joined him along the way to come to a grinding halt in the desert. Kermit is downcast, his dream seems lost, and the integrity that has carried him to this point is on the wane. A second Kermit—his conscience, perhaps—appears, and Kermit

> At some point, you need to answer the call that God has placed upon you and you alone. You have gifts, abilities, and dreams that no one else has.

begins speaking to himself as he struggles with his emotions and what to do at this bump in his journey.

He feels miserable, believing that he has let everyone down. His conscience points out that he would also be miserable if he had stayed in the swamp, never setting out in pursuit of the dream. But he's now worried that in addition to his struggles in the desert, he has brought misfortune upon "a lady pig, a bear, and a chicken, a dog, a thing—whatever Gonzo is. He's a little like a turkey."

Kermit then realizes that the person he made his initial promise to was himself. He set out to accomplish something bigger than himself, and the others came because they believed in the dream.

"To make millions happy." Kermit's integrity and the integrity of the dream required that Kermit stay the course. And at the end of that scene, Kermit comes to that realization.

But the conversation he has with himself when his car breaks down in the desert rings true on other levels. We will always have doubts. Nothing in life is easy, and we will second-guess our quest at critical times. Wherever we aren't seems preferable to where we are—we forget that it was a swamp.

Things change. Life throws us curveballs. Some days it feels like we're facing blitz after blitz. People walk out of our lives or let us down. Things get confusing, loved ones misunderstand us, and relationships become tense. Fear comes and grasps us by the back of the neck, ready to carry us off and away from our dreams. And it often happens when our cars blow up in the desert, or our lives take detours that we didn't plan for, or we get pummeled by disappointments, heartaches, and tragedies. But through it all, the dreams that God put in your heart never change. Your integrity—your promise to yourself—demands that you step up and follow those dreams to a better place, to pick yourself up yet again and push on.

CHAPTER 22
CREATING BALANCE

For disappearing acts, it's hard to beat what happens to the eight hours supposedly left after eight of sleep and eight of work.

DOUG LARSON

SELF-DISCIPLINE IS WHAT LAUREN AND I are trying to teach our children, and it's a part of why I prefer to give our players as much latitude as possible. We are better as a team, and they are better as people, when they can learn to govern themselves and remain accountable to themselves and the mission of the team. It's really an issue of self-control.

I struggle with administering discipline, especially when it comes to disciplining my children. I want to correct their behavior, but more than that, I want them to see that there are negative consequences for certain actions so they can begin to discipline themselves. That's the ultimate goal. I try to achieve a balance so that I get their attention without disciplining so harshly that it overwhelms the lesson or turns them against me.

My parents both had that ability to strike a balance

between the level of punishment and the lesson to be learned. From them I learned that every situation was unique, but that I would face consequences for every wrong action. Even when I was mad about the punishment, deep down I still understood that they wanted the best for me and were trying to teach me something that would help me in the long run. I had to accept the punishment, learn, and grow from it. They tailored our punishments to each of our personalities in order to make sure they got through to us if we didn't meet their expectations. For me, that usually meant the loss of privileges, often involving sports. Instead of being able to go outside, I might have had to stay in and do jobs around the house. I enjoyed the freedom of doing the things that I wanted to do, so losing that privilege was painful. And very effective.

I still remember the talks. "When you can control yourself like an adult and do the things you are expected to do, then you will be allowed to do the things you want to do."

It's really no different once you become an adult, except that you need to be able to control yourself without the direct influence of others, like your parents. No matter what age you are, the same premise my parents taught me holds true: when you can learn to discipline yourself to do what you need to do, you will be allowed to do what you want to do. For most young people, a light will go on at some point as they reach this state of understanding.

People often asked how it was that even though I am not a "disciplinarian," our team played in such a disciplined manner. I think it was because of our desire to pay attention to details and not take anything for granted. We asked players to do their jobs exactly as they should be done and to take ownership for doing them well. Doing things the right way and following through on what you are supposed to do is the difference between being a championship team and being a mediocre one. Reaching those different personalities in the way they can understand, while at the same time helping them to grow as people and learn to discipline themselves, is a necessary skill in coaching.

That is how I have been able to create margins in my life and strike a balance between the things I have to do and those I want to do. I strive to manage my time so that when the day's responsibilities are complete, I can head home. If I work hard and get my work done, I can go home knowing that I have given my employer my best. If I am diligent when I am at home about being present for Lauren and my children, then I can leave with a clear conscience and right relationships when it is time to go back to the office.

> When you can learn to discipline yourself to do what you need to do, you will be allowed to do what you want to do.

The two biggest obstacles I have seen to creating margins in our lives are poor time management and workaholism. The former keeps you from ever feeling like you can allow yourself to leave the office, while the latter is a function of misaligned priorities, a distorted self-image, or some combination of both.

I know many men who have professional achievement as their main priority: climbing the corporate ladder all the way to the top. For some of these men, it probably flows from a sense that this will make them more valuable as men—or at least *seem* more valuable to themselves and others. They see themselves in terms of the respect, the status, or possibly the power that they hope to achieve through the job. Still others probably have an inadequate and unfinished image of themselves, and they believe—subconsciously at times—that more work helps them to be complete. They see themselves as the determined, diligent, committed worker, and therefore spend too many hours at the office trying to fulfill that image they have created.

For the great majority, however, I would suspect that the inability to prioritize and work through tasks during the day is the single biggest impediment to having enough time to do the things they would like to do.

Doing things the right way all the time is the hallmark of a good team, and the cornerstone of a balanced life.

PART VI

CHOOSE
INFLUENCE
OVER IMAGE

I always wondered why
somebody doesn't do
something about that.
Then I realized that
I was somebody.
LILY TOMLIN

KEYS FOR CHOOSING INFLUENCE OVER IMAGE

1. Earning the respect of others starts with the way you treat others.

2. Respect others for their character, not status.

3. Sex comes with consequences. Save it for marriage.

4. You have platforms that are unique to you. Remember that, and change lives around you.

5. You are a role model to someone. Be aware of that and be a good example.

CHAPTER 23

RESPECT FOR YOURSELF AND OTHERS

Men are respectable only as they respect.

RALPH WALDO EMERSON

A LOT OF PEOPLE SEEM to believe that respect is a right, something they are entitled to upon birth. Instead, we need to recognize that respect is something you earn because of your character.

Power, position, stuff, bling—these are the sources from which too many guys think respect comes. I'm concerned that when we do show respect, we're not even respecting the things that we really should. A generation or two ago, we respected honesty, being a good provider for your family, being involved in civic organizations and church, or being a good worker in any honest occupation.

When Art Rooney Sr. was alive, he lived on the north side of Pittsburgh. As the owner of the Steelers, he would walk to the stadium every day, and people always looked out for him and his house, even as the neighborhood got rougher and many others moved out. Rooney never moved, but he continued to treat everyone the way he always had. Rooney knew everyone in our organization, from stars like Terry Bradshaw to the bottom-of-the-roster guys like me. He knew the secretaries and cleaning staff by name, and he made it clear that they were all important to the success of the team. Similarly, the people of Pittsburgh knew that he cared about them and their well-being, and that the Steelers were a community trust, cared for by the Rooneys. What he demonstrated day after day at the office, in his neighborhood, and in the larger community of Pittsburgh was an authentic and sincere respect for all those whom his life touched and who touched his life.

> **Respect is something you earn because of your character.**

One year, the sanitation workers in Pittsburgh went on strike. As I recall, trash was piling up everywhere around the city except in front of Art Rooney's home. As it turns out, some of the workers were picking up his trash on their own. They didn't have to do it. They just wanted to pick up the trash for a man who had always demonstrated a caring interest in them and so many others. A man who had shown them respect.

True respect starts with the way you treat others, and it is earned over a lifetime of acting with kindness, honor, and dignity.

CHAPTER 24

SEXUAL INTEGRITY

Instruction in sex is as important as instruction in food; yet not only are our adolescents not taught the physiology of sex, but never warned that the strongest sexual attraction may exist between persons so incompatible in tastes and capacities that they could not endure living together for a week much less a lifetime.

GEORGE BERNARD SHAW

WE NEED TO BE MORE up-front about sex and its effect on our lives as men. I believe that any sex outside of marriage is wrong. Most of us would agree that infidelity while you're married is wrong, but I'm confident we wouldn't get a consensus on sex before marriage. You may not agree with biblical views of sex outside of marriage, but I'm sure you're at least aware of the problems it's causing in our society.

There are three basic reasons behind my conclusion that even sex before marriage is a bad idea, which I'll tackle in order: it impacts our relationships, it can have physical consequences, and it goes against God's plan.

I think the popular media do us a real disservice in

the area of addressing the emotional consequences of sex outside of marriage. In many romantic comedies or dramas these days, a natural part of building any romantic relationship is sleeping together. And those movies and television shows are very effective, creating an emotional connection between the viewers and the characters so that we're actually happy for the on-screen lovers when it happens.

I think the reality is something quite different. Because of its intimacy—or what *should* be its intimacy—sex can negatively impact a relationship that might otherwise have had a chance to grow into a solid friendship and possibly a marriage. And that should be the goal of dating: friendship, and then, when you've found your soul mate, marriage.

Why sabotage the potential of this relationship or future ones for a few moments of pleasure? This falls into that same category that comes up so many times in being a true man today: learning to defer gratification.

As George Bernard Shaw's quote at the beginning of the chapter reminds us, sex does not assure that two people will grow closer together. Too often with young people, it only masks other problems in the relationship.

When I was in college in the 1970s, we had another popular philosopher: the rock singer Meat Loaf. In his classic song "Paradise by the Dashboard Light," he hits the issue of premarital "love" right on the head. The song tracks a boy and a girl on a car date, with the boy getting more and more interested in sex—right now. The girl refuses throughout, unless he promises to always love her. Finally, at the end of the song, he gives in and promises to marry her, pledging his undying love—to their regret: "I swore that I would love you to the end of time! / So now I'm praying for the end of time. . . . so I can end my time with you!"

> God created you. Your body is valuable. Don't be casual in what you do with it.

Sex outside of marriage creates another problem for today's men: the issue of absentee fathers. Until you are married and ready to be a father, you are taking a chance that you'll end up being one of those dads who sends support payments and struggles to find quality time with his child. Sure, there are ways to be careful, but why take the chance? Only one method is foolproof and accident proof: just don't do it.

And it's more than just pregnancy. Sex outside of marriage has always involved health risks for both partners. We started with syphilis and gonorrhea in my dad's era, added herpes in my time, and now have HIV in today's culture. What's next? We don't know, but history tells us there will surely be something new in the area of sexually transmitted diseases.

Sex outside of marriage also results in spiritual

consequences. We hear a great deal of talk that girls should stay sexually pure so they can wear white on their wedding day. Why isn't there the same focus on boys' staying pure? For some reason, there is a stigma on women who have a lot of sexual partners, but society seems to look at it differently when it comes to men. We've allowed ourselves to be fooled into thinking that it's acceptable because "that's what men do."

But the Bible tells us to "run from sexual sin! No other sin so clearly affects the body as this one does. For sexual immorality is a sin against your own body" (1 Corinthians 6:18). God created you. Your body is valuable. Don't be casual in what you do with it—don't give it away.

Finally, be vigilant with your thoughts and what goes into your mind. Pornography is one of the largest industries on the Internet, which makes it easy for men to bring it right into their homes, where it will quickly gain a foothold if we aren't careful. Whether it creeps in through magazines, television, or the computer, the best way to avoid an addiction to pornography is to avoid the stuff altogether.

Addiction to pornography is just as real as an addiction to alcohol or other drugs, and it can be just as damaging. Like other addictions, it often starts in a subtle way. You don't have to find yourself at an adult bookstore or an X-rated movie to be tempted or led down the path. Today, there are so many avenues where we might find ourselves confronted with those impure thoughts. And even if we think we are mature enough to recognize them and filter them out, what about those who look up to us? If I put the *Sports Illustrated* swimsuit issue on my coffee table, what message am I imprinting on my twelve-year-old's mind?

As with any other addictive substance, you can't be too careful with sexually explicit materials. The next time you're tempted to look, keep this in mind: I have friends who are involved in organizations that are trying to combat the global epidemic of human trafficking. They tell me there's a good chance that the person you're staring at is quite likely a runaway or slave, and that sultry smile is probably forced, hiding a life of incredible pain and hopelessness. Just don't go there.

It takes a strong man to be willing to follow this path of sexual purity, a much stronger man than the one who takes the easy way out and acts on what feels good at the time.

Joe Ehrmann is an assistant coach for a Baltimore-area high school. He was previously a defensive tackle for the Colts, back when they played in Baltimore. I had Joe speak to our team during a recent off-season because I really appreciate his refreshingly candid view on what it takes to be a man. He believes that one of the areas in which the world currently evaluates men is their number of sexual conquests. I think he's right.

And I think that's too bad.

It's too bad for the men and the young men they will influence, for our women and our young ladies, and for our society. The idea that men are somehow to be valued for their sexual prowess is not a new phenomenon; it has been with us for as long as I can remember. I see it with athletes on every level, starting in high school and continuing all the way up to the professional ranks. Male athletes are supposed to have a lot of women. It goes with the territory—and if you don't, people wonder what's wrong with you. It's hard not to buy into that way of thinking when you are immersed in such an environment.

If your convictions, for whatever reason, are that you shouldn't have sex outside of marriage, you're going to face a lot of questions, sometimes even ridicule. It takes a very strong man today to hold up under that kind of pressure.

If you aren't yet married, focus on positive relationships grounded in friendship, and stand firm in the knowledge that you are man enough without notches in your bedpost. There are too many reasons to wait. And being willing to be evaluated on a different scorecard is part of being an uncommon man.

CHAPTER 25

PLATFORMS

Do all the good you can, by all the means you can, in all the ways you can, . . . to all the people you can, for as long as you ever can.

JOHN WESLEY

TOO OFTEN WE LOOK TO others to impact the world, or we decide that we'll wait until later. *Later*, we tell ourselves, *I'll have more free time, money, recognition.* Or we don't think we have the expertise. No one would listen to us. Perhaps what needs to be done is too big, and we don't know where to begin.

A father called me not too long ago. His son's fiancée had died, and he was concerned about his son, who appeared to be slipping into depression as the wedding date approached.

I called the young man, counseled him, and encouraged him that things would get better. We talked a few times and eventually got past the date when he would have been married. I could tell he was beginning to push through the dark clouds. He still hurt but was coming out of the despair. He thanked me and told me he would be all right. "By the way," he said, "what is it that you do?" I told him I was a coach. "Oh, cool," he said. "High school or college?"

The point is that he didn't care that I was anybody famous. Whenever we spoke, I was just a guy his dad knew who had lost a son—and who cared enough to call him. I hope you see this point: people don't care who you are or what you do; they care that you care about them.

We all have opportunities to be either "takers" or "givers." Takers receive value from the lives of others around them. We all do that, and we should, to some extent. It helps us become all we can be. But we can't just take! You may not be an NFL player or coach, a Heisman Trophy winner, or a Super Bowl champion. But you have a unique platform, one that can be used to impact lives that no one else can.

> You have a unique platform, one that can be used to impact lives that no one else can.

You stand where no one else stands. It could be behind a barber's chair, on the field, or across the dinner table. You may never know the impact you're having on someone who's looking up to you because of your character, life's work, family life, or maybe just because of your friendship. In those cases, and others to come, you have a platform in the lives of those you touch.

CHAPTER 26

ROLE MODEL

Don't worry that children never listen to you;
worry that they are always watching you.

ROBERT FULGHUM

WE ALL HAVE INFLUENCE. WE all are role models to someone. We may not want to admit it, we may not want to be, and we may even feel we aren't worthy. But someone is definitely looking up to us.

John Stallworth had joined the Steelers three years before I arrived. John played on teams that won four Super Bowls, was named to four Pro Bowls, and was pictured on the cover of *Sports Illustrated*. In 2002, he was elected to the Pro Football Hall of Fame. Even more important, however, is that John is an outstanding person and was, along with several other teammates, critical to my development as a man.

When I arrived in Pittsburgh, I was a good kid who had been raised well and wanted to do right, but I was in a new situation—and new situations seem to make us more susceptible to peer pressure. I certainly was hoping to make the team and fit in.

John was a great role model for me at that time in

my life. He was friendly and engaging and a lot of fun to be around at the stadium; but when practice was over, he headed home. He had a wife and a family, and as soon as he was done with work obligations, he wanted to be with them. Because I looked up to him as a player and as a person, I found myself wanting those things too: a stable home life and interests outside of football. He never talked down to me about it or preached against the guys who ran the streets. He just lived his life, and I watched. And what I saw made a difference.

We learn from many different sources. We model parents and friends, siblings and peers. We model television and movie characters. That's why it's always important to see yourself as a role model. Right or wrong, somebody somewhere is watching you.

Looking back, I see that one of the added blessings of growing up with two parents whose families lived nearby was the benefit I had of the positive influence of my uncles—my dad's brothers. If my dad hadn't been around while I was growing up, they wouldn't have been a part of my life, either. That would've robbed me of half of my relatives. What a loss that would have been.

Just about all of my dad's and my mom's families lived in the Detroit area. Many weekends we would drive to Detroit to spend the night with my relatives, and when I was young, I didn't know who was on my dad's side of the family and who was on my mom's.

My mom's parents had died when I was young, and my mom had grown close to my father's parents. My dad was close to her siblings, too, so my brother and sisters and I could never keep track of who was on which side.

I was able to see firsthand through my parents and their families how to treat my wife, how to relate to children, and how to treat others with respect. I learned the value of hard work and saw that all work was valuable. There was no difference in the way that any of my uncles were viewed, in spite of their varied professions. It was in those formative years, in those informal settings, that I learned that all honest work to support your family is worthwhile.

> **We all are role models to someone.**

I'm not sure that we always see being a role model as part of our job description. We don't see the need to be intentional about it, or maybe we've become gun-shy about our own mistakes and shortcomings. I know some guys think that because they've made so many mistakes, they can't possibly be a role model for other men or boys, which is definitely not true. Some of the best advice I give to young guys is, "Don't make this mistake like I did!" When I admit that I've made mistakes, I am better qualified to explain just how bad the consequences can be.

You're not disqualified because of your mistakes—none of us is perfect. Thank goodness that the men who built into my life—my dad, my Little League baseball coach, my barber, my teachers—didn't think that way. They made themselves available to me, and I watched and imitated them and learned. I watched the older kids who were in high school when I was young. I watched them practice and imitated them. Fortunately for me, there were some good guys at the high school, guys who weren't too self-centered to help the "little kid," and the things they modeled were beneficial to me. My guess is that they'd had some older guys who did the same for them. So those of you in high school, remember that there are younger kids who think you are special, whether you realize it or not. Be careful of what you do and say.

That's even more critical today as more and more children are growing up without a father in the home. If you and I aren't there to build into their lives, who is going to fill that void? We have to be willing to be intentional and step into their space, whether it's spending time outside or playing video games or sharing their interests. We can't afford to have a vacuum of positive role models. Remember, everyone is a role model, but not everyone is a positive role model. So be intentional and be a good role model. Our kids need you. Some of us adults need you too.

PART VII

LIVE
YOUR FAITH

If you read history you will find that
the Christians who did most for
the present world were precisely
those who thought most of the
next. It is since Christians have
largely ceased to think of the other
world that they have become so
ineffective in this.
C. S. LEWIS

KEYS FOR LIVING YOUR FAITH

1. Remember that you were created by God in His image, special and unique. There is no one else like you, and that's good.

2. Accept a relationship with Christ as your Savior and Lord.

3. Watch over your heart. To watch over your heart, recognize that you can't do it alone. You need to read the Bible and pray.

4. Know that you are going to fall short. You will make mistakes, but you can pick yourself up and press on.

5. Remember that faith involves a knowledge that God will make all things work together for the good of those who love Him, whether we can see it or not.

6. Keep seeking God's purpose for your life. Remember that whatever He has placed in your heart is bigger than you.

7. Remember that God requires you to be faithful, not successful. If you do, you will end up being both—in His eyes.

CHAPTER 27

ETERNAL SELF-ESTEEM

How precious are your thoughts about me, O God.
They cannot be numbered! I can't even count them;
they outnumber the grains of sand!

PSALM 139:17-18

SO MANY OF THE THINGS I have discussed in this book flow from a healthy sense of self-esteem. If there were only one thing I could leave you with, it would be the understanding that you were created by God. Before you were even born, God knew who you would be. Your abilities, interests, and passions are combined within you in a way that has never been seen before. You are unique, and that is good. That's the way God intended it to be.

God doesn't sleep, and He cares for you. God knows your needs and your desires before you even ask. He cares about you in your day-to-day living, in your excitement and grief, in your ups and downs.

Stop and think about that for a minute. I don't know what you've experienced or how those experiences have made you feel about yourself, but after reading those words—that *God cares about you in every circumstance*—do you think about yourself differently? I believe that God cares about all of us—He cares about me and about you.

I am concerned about kids who never come to believe that about themselves, who see themselves as cosmic accidents. If life is seen as accidental, then wasting my life, or taking someone else's, may not be a big deal. We have already gone too far in that direction.

I am troubled by a society that devalues life directly and insidiously and then markets that idea to kids through video games, music, movies, and television. This, in turn, contributes to kids' not realizing that life should be respected, nurtured, and protected. The summer of 2008 was the worst three-month stretch in the history of the city of Indianapolis in terms of homicides. Most of the suspects were young men, men who probably didn't see life as having value or as being something that God cares about. And with each killing, we actually lost two people: the victim, gone from this world, and the perpetrator, who may ultimately be sentenced to prison. Somehow we've got to reverse this trend, and I think it starts with getting people to see themselves as God sees them.

> **I believe that God cares about all of us–He cares about me and about you.**

Life is precious and should be viewed as such. You were created by God.

CHAPTER 28

RELATIONSHIP WITH CHRIST

God blesses those who are poor and realize their need for him, for the Kingdom of Heaven is theirs.

MATTHEW 5:3

THE BIBLE SAYS, "GOD BLESSES those who . . . realize their need for him."

He wants you to spend eternity with Him in heaven. It's pretty clear in the Scriptures that the way to ensure this is to recognize that you need Him. None of us is perfect, and because of our sin (falling short of God's standard for our lives), we are separated from Him. Without being holy, like God, we cannot be in a right relationship with Him—without something else occurring.

God has provided that "something else" in the person of His Son, Jesus Christ. God loved us so much that He sent His only Son to earth to die for us and take the punishment for our sinful nature, so that we could have a direct relationship with Christ and God. And all we have to do is desire to be in a relationship with God, understand that we can't do it ourselves, and believe that God sent His Son for us.

It's a free gift from God.

When we believe that in our hearts and accept Jesus Christ as our Savior (He died on the cross for us) and our Lord (making Him the number-one priority in our lives), then we are assured of spending eternity with Him in heaven (see John 3:16-17).

For Jesus, the heart is where everything begins. Our heart reflects to the world who we are—the inner character that we display outwardly. The quarterback of the soul, it guides the decisions we make along the way and determines what we will leave behind us along the journey's path. Our heart sets the course of every day of our lives.

Jesus often spoke of the condition of our hearts. At one juncture, He was speaking to a group of religious leaders, those who were very careful to follow all the religious laws. His comments to them cut to their cores:

> *You brood of snakes! How could evil men like you speak what is good and right? For whatever is in your heart determines what you say. A good person produces good things from the treasury of a good heart, and an evil person produces evil things from the treasury of an evil heart. (Matthew 12:34-35)*

When it comes to protecting the heart and keeping it pure, a few strategies have helped me. First, be careful what you put into your mind. The things that we dwell on or fill our minds with will often come bubbling back up whether we want them to or not.

Second, fill yourself with God's Word by reading it. There are a lot of great books you can read, books with positive messages that will help you. But I don't think there is anything that will help you as much as hearing directly from God, and that's what you're doing when you read the Bible. A lot of young people tell me that the Bible is hard to understand, but a modern translation can help. Most often, I use a translation written in the English we speak today, as opposed to the "King's English" of many centuries ago. My Bible even has study notes; Scripture includes enough challenging passages, so I'll take all the help I can get.

Finally, stay in prayer. Pray alone, and pray with others, too, including your girlfriend or wife, and your children, if you have any. If you're a young person and your parents have never prayed with you—or haven't prayed with you lately—ask them to. This may feel awkward at first, but it will help bring you closer to God and closer to each other. Just remember that prayer is

> For Jesus, the heart is where everything begins. Our heart sets the course of every day of our lives.

simply having a conversation with God. There are no rules or special words.

The depth and quality of our relationship with Jesus Christ are governed by the state of our hearts. It will reveal the reasons why we do what we do.

We need to make sure that what we do in church or in our community is done for Christ and not for our own prestige and acceptance. Are your prayer and Bible reading done simply to fulfill expectations or out of a sincere desire to find God, learn more about Him, and discover what He wants for your life?

In our relationships, the state of our hearts will reveal how we view those around us. Do we see our wives and children simply as "wives" and "children," associating them with all the usual responsibilities expected of us, or do we see them as special creations of God, His precious children whom He has entrusted to our care?

Do we see the burdens of friendships or the blessings of friendships?

Do we really believe that we were uniquely created by a God who loves us and walks with us?

The Bible says, "God blesses those whose hearts are pure," and then offers this great promise: "for they will see God."

CHAPTER 29

FAITH

It's faith in something and enthusiasm for something that makes a life worth living.

OLIVER WENDELL HOLMES

WE DON'T CONTROL EVERYTHING.

That's difficult for us to admit sometimes, but I think that's central to some of the issues that plague us as men. I have young children who look to me to make sure that nothing bad will ever happen to them; I tell myself I'm doing just that. And I make sure they know that too. I am ever vigilant in protecting them.

I was tucking in Jade, my younger daughter, recently. We had said her prayers, and I pulled the covers up and bent down to give her a kiss.

She hugged my neck, pulled me toward her, and whispered into my ear, "Keep me safe while I'm asleep, okay?"

"Of course I will, sweetheart."

And I meant it. The reality is that we do all that we can, but our best efforts to control the world will always fall short. As one of more than six billion people on the planet, I can't possibly think I'm in charge of it all.

Therefore, I am summoning faith all the time: Faith in the belief that gravity will bring me back down the next time I jump. Faith that the pilot of the flight I'm on won't fall asleep in the front when I do in the back. Faith that whoever programmed the traffic signals set the other side to red when mine shows green. Faith that my children will come home safely when the school day is over.

> **Our lives will be more effective if we live according to God's game plan rather than trying to take matters into our own hands.**

We use faith all the time in football as well. Our Cover 2 defense requires a great deal of faith, and it can take players quite a while to get acclimated. Some never do. Because the defense is so assignment oriented, our players need to have trust and faith for it to work. They aren't allowed to free-lance and simply run to the ball. They have to protect their areas, stay in their gaps, and trust the system. They have to trust that everyone else will do his particular assignment and have faith that if that occurs, the defense will be effective.

It's much more instinctive to run immediately to the ball. It's that control thing we have within us. We want to control everything, make every play, be everywhere on the field. All players do that by nature, I think, but most can be coached to read their key and go to the spot that key tells them to go to, whether the ball appears to be going there or not. Those are the players we need. The ones that have a hard time believing that the overall defense is better even if they aren't personally in the thick of the play really can't help us.

Offense requires faith as well. Peyton Manning throws most of his passes to a set spot before the receiver has made his final break. He has to have faith that the receiver will run the proper route and arrive at that spot when the ball gets there. The receiver has to have faith that if he runs his route at the proper depth and with the proper speed, the ball will be thrown to the spot where he can catch it.

Life works the same way. We can act like we're in control, or that we've got things figured out, but Jesus was clear that we are not promised tomorrow. Only God knows how everything will play out. And our lives will be more effective if we live according to His game plan rather than trying to take matters into our own hands. Paul wrote in his letter to the Romans that "in all things God works for the good of those who love him" (Romans 8:28, NIV). This doesn't mean that everything will work out the way we hope, but that God has everything in His sights, and that He will cause everything to work together for *His* purpose. In *His* time. Our problems, our worries, our sins, and our pain will all work together in God's time and for God's purpose.

And that is where faith comes in. Some things are beyond our comprehension. Some days—or years— it seems as if nothing is going right, and we get on a losing streak. Our teenage children don't listen to us, and they behave in ways that worry us. Our marriages may be going through a desert, where things just aren't what we thought they would be. Our coaches, our teachers, our parents, or our bosses may be acting unreasonably or treating us unfairly.

Even in the face of all those circumstances, God is there. God is with you, every step of the way, and He knows where this is all headed.

As for me, I know that I can't make it through life relying solely on my own smarts and strength. Life is too tough, and too many things come up that I have no control over. Some people try to fool themselves into thinking that self-reliance is possible, but it really is foolish to think we don't have to have faith in anyone or anything else. It's also a lonely way to go through life.

And it leaves out the perspective of eternal life.

CHAPTER 30

PURPOSE

What if there's something bigger for me out there
Than the comfort of a life on this middle ground?
I've played it safe but now I can't help but wonder
If maybe I've been missing out
I want to finally take the road less traveled
I want to run away from anything typical
I want the world to see the life I'm living
And call it uncommon.

MATTHEW WEST, "UNCOMMON"

I BELIEVE THAT GOD KNEW that you would be where you are in right now, with the passions, gifts, and platform that only you have. I believe the imprint you are meant to leave on this world is not accidental or coincidental. Your life has been intentionally designed by God to have a uniquely significant and eternal impact on the world around you. What if we all lived our lives embracing that idea as true—what would our lives begin to look like?

I believe first and foremost that I operate from God's grace. That grace is not a license to do whatever I choose but rather an understanding that despite my best efforts, I will fall short in my striving for

God, and that's okay. When it happens, I get up, dust myself off, and press on toward the mark.

And as I press on, I am called to ask, "What kind of world do I want?" Anyone can complain, but I need to be prepared to offer thoughts on how I can improve myself, my home, my town, my country, and the world.

> Your life has been intentionally designed by God to have a uniquely significant and eternal impact on the world around you.

We have all seen people less fortunate than us, who seem to have little hope for anything to change without external intervention. We have all been saddened as we watched people in less developed countries die from starvation or disease for want of food, medicine, or other things that we take for granted. We may not be able to solve these problems ourselves—but we do have our own passions and abilities, and we can begin to make a difference today.

We're not always going to reach those things we really desire; in fact, failure may happen more often than not. But we can find peace and happiness in the knowledge that we're striving within our real purpose that honors God. If we're striving only for ourselves, then we'll be dissatisfied, always yearning for more, while the world waits.

Strive instead within a purpose—your purpose—that honors God.

CHAPTER 31
SIGNIFICANCE

Success is to be measured not so much by the position that one has reached in life as by the obstacles which he has overcome.

BOOKER T. WASHINGTON

I THINK OUR SCORECARD IS wrong. I'm more inclined to agree with Chuck Noll's way of thinking: that our success on Sundays wasn't always measured by the stadium scoreboard. There were games in which we played very well but had fewer points at the end. To most, we were losers. Or maybe we played poorly yet won. To most, we were winners. Chuck would rather have played well and lost than played poorly and won.

It's easy to fall into the trap of looking at the wrong scorecard. We decide that a head coach, a CEO, a celebrity, or a billionaire is significant. I don't think so. Those people might *have* significance, but it's not simply because of their position or resources. Significance is a much deeper issue than that.

Have you figured out what God has placed you here to do, and are you doing it to the best of your abilities? Therein lies the answer to significance.

It's a liberating place to be once you figure it out. I was fortunate enough to coach a team to a Super Bowl win and reach what is recognized as the pinnacle of my profession. But it never has been an all-encompassing quest for me. I realized that while winning the Super Bowl was something we were striving for, it was not going to make my life complete if we won— and not winning it would not ruin my life.

God calls us to be faithful, not successful.

Instead, I tried to focus at each stop along the way on those priorities I had already decided were important: being a good coach, learning enough to become a better one, and spending my free time with my family and in ministry opportunities. I wanted to win. I still do. God wired me to be competitive.

The best measuring stick of that competitive nature, however, is whether we are true to the call in our heart and act on that call to the best of our abilities.

God didn't create your life to be a series of accidents and coincidences. He knew before you were born that you would be where you are today. He knew that you would have the influence over those you do, and He already knows those you will impact down the line. Through it all, the legacy you leave will determine what your life on earth meant.

Nathan, my coauthor, was giving a talk in Boston.

He told the audience about his experience in trying to become an author, or more specifically, trying to talk me into writing *Quiet Strength*. He told of the ups and downs and despairs of the journey and the times when he thought he should give up. A friend along the way told him that until God clearly closed the door, he should continue with his dream. He did.

Finally, I agreed to write *Quiet Strength*, and a new set of challenges appeared. Some publishers wanted me to use a proven writer, not a first-timer like Nathan. Others were concerned about the tight deadline we had. We were forewarned that sports books generally don't sell well. We were told how many books are written each year and that most sell fewer than ten thousand copies.

Nathan concluded his talk by giving statistics on the book, including best-seller rankings on the most prestigious lists and sales of over one million. Then he tied these things to Proverbs 16:3: "Commit your actions to the LORD, and your plans will succeed."

Nathan pointed out that the verse doesn't say exactly when we can expect success but that success *will* come in the Lord's time. He also noted how God's plans are so much bigger than ours. Nathan's main goal three years earlier had been merely to *write* a book, without really giving much thought to how it might sell once it was published.

After the talk, a friend took Nathan aside and told him that he thought Nathan's conclusion was wrong.

"You're using the world's measuring sticks—sales numbers and best-seller lists—to measure whether or not the book was a success. I watched you bang your head against a wall for three years; that, to me, is a success, whether the book ever came into existence or sold any copies at all," he told him.

My scorecard is slightly different. By the time I decided to go ahead with *Quiet Strength*, publishers were interested, so we knew a book would result. But we had no idea how well it would do. What God wants me to remember, though, is that in His eyes, success is measured by lives changed, not sales numbers.

God calls us to be faithful, not successful. He calls us to follow those dreams in our hearts and to pursue them with all our might. Sometimes they will proceed in ways that make them a "success" in worldly terms, but other times it may feel more like futility. Sometimes we'll be able to witness changed lives, and sometimes the only life we see changed is our own.

God's scorecard is different from ours. He does want to bless us, but His scorecard doesn't use money or material possessions or fame or status. He judges by the state of our hearts and our desire to serve Him.

Don't ever sell yourself short. God's purposes are greater than man's purposes. There is much to do and much that you are capable of doing. Start now to be uncommon.

A FINAL WORD

Everybody can be great . . . because anybody can serve. You don't have to have a college degree to serve. You don't have to make your subject and verb agree to serve. You only need a heart full of grace, a soul generated by love.

MARTIN LUTHER KING JR.

LIFE IS ALL ABOUT THE journey. We pay so much attention to where we are going or what we have accomplished that we sometimes forget to appreciate where we are and how we've gotten to this point.

As I write this, Brandon Robinson is in the tenth year of his twenty-eight-year sentence. After attending a chapel service in prison, he accepted Christ into his life, and it had a huge impact on him. He got his high school diploma, his bachelor's degree, and an MBA while in prison. As part of his community-service requirement, he has been allowed to speak to young people about the mistakes he's made. He has a powerful testimony. I have had him speak to our team not only about the dangers of drinking and driving but also about the dangers of falling into that lifestyle, and his talk has had more impact on our players than anything I could say. He has contacted the accident victims' families and been forgiven by some of them. But no matter how hard he tries, he will never forget the bad decisions that led to that terrible night or be able to erase their consequences.

Dallas Clifton is in the second year of his sentence, and he, too, is taking classes in prison. He hopes to go back to school when he's released. It's been difficult for him, knowing the pain he has caused his mom and sisters. Prison life isn't easy, but it does give time to reflect on the decisions made and those that will be made in the future. And he, too, wishes he could change them.

But life is like football in that once a play is run, you don't get a chance to do it over. The only thing you can do is move forward and try to make the situation better. I really believe both Dallas and Brandon are going to do that.

Like Brandon and Dallas, we sometimes decide to follow the crowd, and the results make us feel like our journey has hit a dead end. Remember this: God has created you different from anyone else. You have gifts and abilities that I don't have, and I probably have some that you don't. But we are both of infinite value in God's eyes, and both of us are capable of so much more than the world says we are.

We aren't supposed to play by the world's rules. The world has systematically changed the values of the important things in life, switching them with those that don't matter at all. Those things that are truly valuable have been discounted to ridiculous levels, while meaningless things have been held in the highest esteem.

When our family travels from Indianapolis to Tampa, we often fly Southwest Airlines. One of the fascinating things to me about Southwest is that they have been successful by going against the norm. They did away with assigned seating, ignored major metropolitan airports, and cut their maintenance and training costs by having only one type of aircraft. They didn't do it everybody else's way. At times, I'm sure Southwest's leaders felt like they were standing alone, telling stockholders, "This will work. Trust us."

But it's okay to stand alone: "Don't copy the behavior and customs of this world, but let God transform you into a new person by changing the way you think. Then you will learn to know God's will for you, which is good and pleasing and perfect" (Romans 12:2).

While everyone is racing around, trying to figure out how to get ahead in terms of worldly status and success, keep playing a different game.

Start now. Be *Uncommon*.

ABOUT THE AUTHORS

TONY DUNGY is the #1 *New York Times* bestselling author of *Quiet Strength, Uncommon, The Mentor Leader,* and *The One Year Uncommon Life Daily Challenge.* He led the Indianapolis Colts to Super Bowl victory on February 4, 2007, the first such win for an African American head coach. Dungy established another NFL first by becoming the first head coach to lead his teams to the playoffs for ten consecutive years. He joined the Colts in 2002 after serving as the most successful head coach in Tampa Bay Buccaneers history. He has also held assistant coaching positions with the University of Minnesota, Pittsburgh Steelers, Kansas City Chiefs, and Minnesota Vikings. Before becoming a coach, Dungy played three seasons in the NFL. He retired from coaching in 2009 and now serves as a studio analyst for NBC's *Football Night in America.* He and his wife, Lauren, are the parents of seven children.

NATHAN WHITAKER is the coauthor of *Quiet Strength, Uncommon, The Mentor Leader,* and *The One Year Uncommon Life Daily Challenge* and a Harvard Law School graduate whose firm currently represents NFL and college coaches and administrators. A two-sport athlete in baseball and football at Duke University, he has worked in football administration for the Jacksonville Jaguars and Tampa Bay Buccaneers. He lives in Florida with his wife, Amy, and their two daughters.

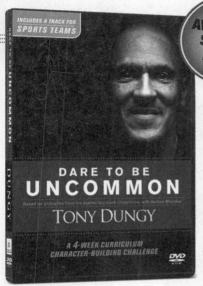

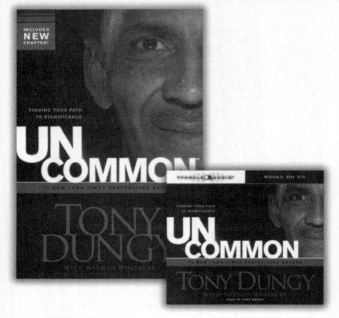

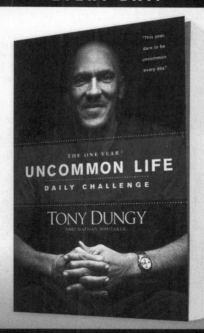

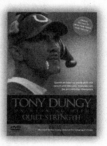
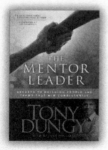